Praise for You 1, Anxiety 0

Jodi Aman, author of *You 1, Anxiety 0* offers in the pages of this marvelous book, the hope of rediscovering your inner beauty and serenity. She shares her wisdom by weaving salient suggestions and her life-altering recommendations into a compelling narrative, one that artfully includes insightful stories of some of her most interesting clients. The skills and tactics offered in this must read self-help book, *You 1, Anxiety 0* will prove invaluable to you on your quest to better health.

~Terry A. Gordon, MD, author of *No Storm Lasts Forever*

Jodi knows first-hand what it's like to recover from anxiety and fear, so she fully understands what others who suffer from this are going through. Her approach to anxiety recovery is revolutionary … yet easy and logical. I love her practical approach and positive-ly transformational wisdom. If you've ever suffered from anxiety or fear, get her book. It will transform your life!

~Robin Jay, writer/producer, *The Secrets of the Keys*

If you feel that anxiety is running your life, *You 1, Anxiety 0* is a must-read book. Jodi Aman has an incredible talent for helping people with anxiety realize that not only can they gain control over their anxiety, they deserve to be free of anxiety. Filled with real-life examples, easy-to-understand explanations, and action plans, this book breaks down exactly how anxiety wraps its tentacles around you — and how, by understanding its tactics, you can banish it for good.

~J.D. Bailey, HonestMom.com

This is a remarkably pragmatic book that has turned some of the best of narrative therapy practice and directed it at the problem of anxiety. These ideas have turned around the lives of so many peo-ple. To see Jodi translating them into *You 1, Anxiety 0* in such a skillful and imaginative way gives me the greatest joy.

~David Epston, co-author with Michael White of
Narrative Means to Therapeutic Ends

You 1, Anxiety 0 is a book that inspires true, realistic hope. Neither dry and distant nor full of hocus-pocus fluff that turns out to be useless, Aman's book gives readers the encouragement and infor-mation needed to break free from anxiety. Reading this book is like sitting down with Jodi herself on a comfy couch, sun streaming in through the window, sipping tea, and figuring out how to live your life free from anxiety.

~Tanya J. Peterson, MS, author of *My Life in a Nutshell*

This book has given me hope. Hope that I can get my life back on track. I didn't know anxiety was such a self-esteem issue. Very thankful for this book.

~Matt Papas, SurvivingMyPast.net

LOVE this book!! The book is refreshingly powerful and the exer-cises are easy to implement. Jodi deconstructs anxiety and brings the reader into clearly looking at all of the tricks anxiety plays. The end result is peace! This book is a must-read!!

~Corinne Zupko, Author of *From Anxiety to Love*

You 1, Anxiety 0

You 1
Anxiety 0

Win Your
Life Back
from Fear
and Panic

J O D I   A M A N

Creator of the Anxiety-Free Me™
Online Anxiety Recovery Program

Ja'Love Books

Published by: Ja'Love Books
919 S Winton Rd.
Rochester NY 14618

This book is available at quantity discounts for educational use. For further information, please contact author at info@jodiaman.com.

You 1, Anxiety 0 is designed to provide practical recommendations to ease anxiety suffering. It is not meant to replace the medical or mental health advice of your current provider. If further assistance is required, the services of a local competent professional should be sought.

Library of Congress Cataloging-in-Publications Data
Aman, Jodi.
   You 1, Anxiety 0 : win your freedom back from fear and panic / Jodi Aman –Second Edition.
   pages cm
   Include bibliographical references.
ISBN: 978-0-9985613-0-1 (paperback)
ISBN: 978-0-9985613-1-8 (ebook)
1. Anxiety 2. Self Help 3. Mental Health 4. Psychology
                    2017902678

Many names and identifying characteristics of people mentioned in this work have been changed to protect their identities.

To Ted,
my MVP.

Table of Contents

Acknowledgments

I have a deep well of gratitude for so many people: Donna, Tom, Sheree, Samantha, Janice, Sam, Stephanie, Leslie, Jack, Keith, Jessica, Cara, Mary, Jane, Deva, Christopher, Tyler, Paul, Celia, Jamie, Jill, Deborah, Tammy, Betsy, Tim, Mike, Kelly and Tally, who allowed me to share their stories.

Tina Barbour, Ted Aman, and Danielle Scruton for reading my first drafts. Amanda Berlin and Polgarus Studio, for their thorough edits. 1106 Design for the cover design. Renee Hall for the cover photo. Michelle Radomski for the interior formatting. Stephanie Veraghen, who held down the fort. Erin Smith and Carmen Perez, for their encouragement and advice. David Epston for being a kind and assiduous teacher. Dulwich Center for their education and encouragement.

My in-laws, my parents and siblings, for allowing me to bounce ideas off them, and believing in me. And last but not least, my husband, Ted, and our kids, Cal, Leo and Lily, for their patience, steadfast faith and support.

Introduction

Does anxiety take up a large part of your day?

Do you worry about bad things happening to you or to someone you love?

Do you avoid regular activities because of anxiety?

Is it affecting your relationships?

Are you afraid of what people think of you?

If you answer yes to any of these questions, then this book is for you!

I'm not going to minimize the impact anxiety can have on your life because I know firsthand how horrible anxiety feels. I struggled with anxiety and panic for more than two decades. Some days I could barely get out of bed. I was scared of dying, getting sick, being in an accident — you name it; everything and anything terrified me. My panic would last for hours and sometimes for days. I avoided restaurants, social events and traveling. I often couldn't even go into work.

Once I clawed my way out of anxiety and completely cured myself, I began teaching the practical steps I used for my own healing to the clients in my psychotherapy practice. They worked! More and more folks left their anxiety in the dust and were happier than they thought they could be.

During thousands of these therapeutic conversations, I continued to learn extensive details on how anxiety works and how to resist it, and I honed the map to anxiety recovery. With so many men, women and children suffering with anxiety today, I want to spread the message of hope and healing to a larger number than the eight people a day I can see personally in my practice. I wrote this book so it can reach you.

Using the strategies in this book, you can win your life back. I make the steps practical and easy to follow; I provide many, many examples so you can understand and embody what to do at every level — physical, emotional, mental and spiritual. Exercises accompany every section to help guide you along the shortest path to healing from anxiety.

You and I both know how anxiety can destroy a person's life and take away joy, opportunities, and relationships. It can override, delay and destroy your life purpose. My hope is that **You 1, Anxiety 0** will help create a better world by guiding you to free yourself from the struggle of anxiety and find inner peace. Then, you can create family, community and world peace.

In this book, I take you through six keys to moving from fear and panic to complete happiness in your life. In the first three chapters, I share my own journey and explain what fear and anxiety are in order to take away your self-blame and fear. In Chapter 4, I expose 15 tricks and tactics of anxiety to break down the power it has on your life. In Chapter 5, I help you cultivate your control by sharing the 15 most common skills to overcoming anxiety. In the last two chapters I teach you how to let go of unwanted emotions and feelings that feed anxiety, show you why self-compassion is an essential practice for your anxiety recovery, teach you how to strategically use affirmations to change the triggers of your brain and finally share daily practices to keep your mind happy and healthy.

Because these ideas have helped so many people, I'm convinced that this book can help YOU win your freedom back from fear and panic, too.

Anxiety is curable! After reading my book you will

- Understand the biology of anxiety and no longer be afraid of it
- Learn the lies that anxiety tells so you no longer believe them
- Hone your skills and abilities to get rid of anxiety before it surfaces

You can't imagine how good you will feel when you get anxiety out of your life. Let's get started...

This book teaches how to get rid of anxiety from your life.

If you have intense panic and want tips on how to calm yourself down immediately, so that you can focus on healing for good, check out my video

**20 Ways to Calm
from Anxiety and Panic**

find it here:
jodiaman.com/20ways

Pick on Someone Your Own Size

Donna[1] often felt powerless and defeated by anxiety, and believed getting better was "too hard" for her, because despite her every effort she continued to feel this way. She'd heard from a mental health professional that she needed to gain some "coping skills" to learn how to deal with her "generalized anxiety" and "panic disorder."

A problem was that she didn't know how to acquire these skills. This added "feeling like a horrible failure at managing her life" to her already debilitating problems.

Donna was scared to go outside, particularly without her husband, and had trouble facing simple day-to-day tasks such as driving the car. She was desperate for relief, but didn't think recovery was possible and prayed her anxiety would just go away. To compound matters, Donna felt embarrassed in front of her family and friends for being "weak and cowardly."

The crushing anxiety and panic began years earlier when her husband Dave, rapidly losing blood after an accident, was rushed to the hospital. Witnessing large amounts of blood and the doctors and nurses trying to stabilize him in the emergency room was

---

1   Stories are used with permission. The names used have been changed for privacy

incredibly frightening. Donna describes herself that day as being "out of control" as she watched the doctors and nurses revive her husband. She felt faint and overwhelmed. The memory paralyzed her so powerfully that it convinced Donna she couldn't handle anything in life, similar to how she "lost it" that day.

I wasn't convinced. I asked her more about what happened.

What did you do when you felt faint?

What did you do next?

What happened?

As I suspected, she had answers. Donna was quite clear about how she reacted that day, recalling that she sat down when she felt faint. People around her were concerned and she was able to reassure them and drink a glass of water. Donna calmly answered questions about Dave. She did some deep breathing and when it was allowed, Donna checked on her husband.

"Hmmm, I see. You sat down, answered some questions, drank a glass of water and breathed?" I asked.

"Yep," she said.

"All right. Then tell me, at what point were you out of control?"

"The whole time," she said, confused by the question.

I again reminded her, "You had the wherewithal to find a chair and sit down in case you fainted. You were able to speak coherently to answer questions the staff asked about your husband, you drank some water, closed your eyes and concentrated on your breathing. You then checked on your husband and eventually calmed down. You felt awful, understandably, but I'm still wondering when you lost control, because I haven't heard it yet."

There was a silence as Donna considered this. I said, "I mean, did you black out? Was there a moment you can't account for? A period of time when you didn't have control over your actions?"

"No, I remember the whole thing."

I repeated her action steps once more, slowly. Donna's eyes had that faraway look as she listened. Soon, she began to understand.

She'd never thought of it like this. She called it a "revelation" to think that not only did she not lose it, but instead "handled it quite well, considering."

Before she came to see me, Donna had little hope of getting over her anxiety and panic attacks. Since her husband's emergency, she'd been terrified of going to the doctor, fearing losing control again. She was especially afraid of having her blood pressure taken.

It was an upcoming doctor's appointment — where her blood pressure would be taken — that brought Donna to reach out to me. Knowing she would be anxious and it would raise her BP even more caused further panic. In the last year, she'd cancelled or walked out of several appointments.

During our conversation Donna's anxiety shifted, because she no longer saw herself as being out of control on the day of her husband's crisis. By the end of our meeting, Donna was no longer nervous about going to the doctor or about having her blood pressure taken.

A few months later I learned that Donna had gone to the doctor and had her blood pressure taken without incident. Over the following years she suffered no further trouble.

Donna had firm beliefs about her anxiety and disempowering ideas about herself.

- *She thought that she had no control over anxiety.*
- *She thought it was too hard to feel better.*
- *She thought she would be like this forever.*
- *She thought that she couldn't handle hard situations and was terrified of one coming.*
- *She thought that she didn't have enough coping skills.*
- *She thought she was weak and cowardly.*
- *She thought she was a failure at life.*

Do you see anything of yourself in Donna?

The way you think about anxiety — that it's horrible and scary — and the way you think about yourself — that you're weak and a failure — affect you much more than the physical, nervous feelings.

The biggest obstacle to getting over your anxiety is that you feel like you have no control over it. That healing is not possible for you. You've tried everything to make it go away, but the anxiety is still there and it must be your fault. How else can you explain it?

You might be barely keeping your head above water just dealing with anxiety, so you've no energy left to get over it. And you don't see how you can get over it anyway. It's beaten you down so much, you have very little hope that things can be different.

You tell yourself things like, *I've got anxiety. This is just how I'm wired. I have to learn to live with it.*

It must be true, because it feels real and when you've tried to seek professional help you're told, "You've got anxiety. This is how you're wired. You just have to learn to live with it."

Within you, though, there's that gnawing hope, that desperation, for relief. A hope beyond the hopelessness that it will go away and you can breathe and smile again.

Okay, you think. *I have to learn coping skills to calm me when I'm anxious.*

However, this doesn't solve the problem of being anxious in the first place.

You're also embarrassed to be suffering this terrible emotional turmoil, while everyone around you is so normal. This self-judgment feeds your anxiety and snowballs out of control very quickly.

If this describes you, I totally understand. I've been there myself.

In this book I'll explain what fear is and why it can have so much power. I'll help you to break down the beliefs holding you prisoner to anxiety and teach you simple, easy to understand, strategic steps toward getting over your anxieties. I'll put recovery in your reach by showing you how to take power away from the anxiety *before* it comes, putting you back in the driver's seat of your life. And finally, I'll help you to stop judging and start trusting yourself.

Anxiety affects our mind, body and soul. This suffering has stolen your joy, your sense of adventure, your opportunities and practically your very *self*. It's time to take a stand against anxiety and get yourself better. Here's why.

1.   Fear and anxiety have taken up too much of your life.

Anxiety takes loads of energy to sustain, sucking it from other more important things in our lives such as our families, hobbies, joys and everything else that matters to us. This is a waste.

Living free from anxiety can't be delayed. Life is precious and every moment of it counts. It's hard sometimes — probably right now it's hard. But nothing stays the same.

I'll show you how to take control and create the life you want.

2.   It is possible to beat anxiety.

In my twenty years of practicing as a counselor, I've helped people with the worst cases of anxiety get better.

That doesn't mean it's simple or easy. You might be feeling completely overwhelmed. But, because I've seen thousands of people recover from these debilitating thoughts and fears, I know it's possible for you, too. I have complete confidence and hope that there can be calm and peace in your future, no matter how far down the road of fear you've traveled.

Reading this, your mind may be going down one of two paths.

It might be saying, "Oh good, there is hope for me!"

Or, it might be saying, "I'm different. I can't get it. Everyone can feel better, except me."

If your mind takes you down the second path, let that thought go for a moment.

If those people felt *as bad as you* and figured out how to generate happiness after their pain, then it's possible for you, too. Happiness is available after pain. Even for you, no matter how horrible your history or how intense your anxiety, or that you've tried everything already. Anxiety's tactic is having you think that you have no control over it. You need to take back your control.

You've got this. I know you do.

Airline flight attendants tell us that in the case of an emergency we need to put our own oxygen masks on, before assisting others. This is good life advice as well.

When we have anxiety, we put the mask on anxiety first, giving it what it needs to survive (our attention, our fear, isolation) while we're almost asphyxiating ourselves, desperately praying it has mercy on us.

First, exhale. When you feel like you can't breathe, it's often because you're trying to take more air in, but you forgot to breathe out.

Then ask yourself, *Which do I want to nurture, myself or the anxiety?*

3. You don't deserve anxiety.

When you experience trauma or bad times, you sometimes wonder if *you* caused it somehow, or you're left with a deep doubt whether or not something's wrong with you. This makes you feel vulnerable to being hurt again. If it's your fault that bad things happen, then you might conclude that you *deserve* to feel bad, in pain and fearful.

Don't believe that for a moment. Anxiety has nothing to do with what you deserve. Happiness has nothing to do with what you deserve, either. When panic attacks start, you *feel* like a failure — and since you feel like you can't handle life, you decide it must be true that you can't. Your mind takes that baton and continues the self-recrimination. *I'm such a weakling. I am an idiot. I don't deserve to feel better.*

People are so hard on themselves and even take responsibility for other people's actions. If someone betrays you, you spend mental energy trying to figure out how you *allowed it to happen.* You *define* yourself by other people's actions. You see yourself through negative self-judgments — stupid, screw-up, weak, loser and overemotional. Fear and doubt feed off this self-judgment.

Someone hurt you and you blame yourself, because it's the easiest way to make sense of it. The mind does this, because it's influenced by the common belief that people get what they deserve. I don't believe that people get what they deserve — bad things happen to good people all the time. They don't deserve it. And neither do you.

You deserve to win your freedom back from anxiety. You deserve to be happy and free to make choices without anxiety getting in the way.

4. It is not as hard as you think.

> *Whether you think you can,*
> *or you think you can't —*
> *you're right.*
> ~Henry Ford

"Hard" is relative. Effort feels different at different times, and different to different people. But when you say or think, *It's too hard,* you're deciding this before you know how hard it will be. It's disheartening and becomes an obstacle in your path.

The practices I suggest are not hard. They will take commitment, attention and energy. But believe me, it's a lot easier than feeling anxious all the time. Living with anxiety has had you doing many, many hard things. Feeling better will be a cinch compared to that.

None of us are strangers to the idea that it takes effort to accomplish things. The inherent challenge in that effort sparks our interest and enthusiasm. Humans love challenges and feel invigorated by them. Challenges help us grow and feel alive. They connect us with our abilities and give us confidence.

You can do this. I believe in you.

5. It's time.

- It's time to break the binds of fear.
- It's time to stop being afraid.
- It's time to rule your own life instead of feeling like you're ruled by your anxiety.
- It's time to feel happy and present in your relationships.
- It's time to reclaim your joy.

Take Action

Contemplate what you'll discover as you move past anxiety.

- Loving and connecting with people can enrich your life.
- Taking risks is more exciting than avoiding great opportunities.
- Reaching out is more satisfying than letting heartfelt words go unspoken.
- "Protecting" usually equals suffering.
- Living free beats living in fear any day of the week.
- Control is a matter of perception.
- Peace is available to anyone, even someone living in oppression. Make a list of the many cool things you can do when you're not restricted by anxiety. By the time you finish this book, you'll be able to do plenty!

If anxiety didn't stop me, I would...

_____

_____

_____

_____

_____

_____

_____

_____

_____

_____

_____

_____

_____

_____

Sorry Anxiety,
You Lose!

This guy's walking down the street when he falls in a hole. The walls are so steep he can't get out.

A doctor passes by and the guy shouts up, "Hey, you! Can you help me out?" The doctor writes a prescription, throws it down in the hole and moves on.

Then a priest comes along and the guy shouts up, "Father, I'm down in this hole. Can you help me out?" The priest writes out a prayer, throws it down the hole and moves on

Then a friend walks by. "Hey, Joe, it's me. Can you help me out?" And the friend jumps in the hole. Our guy says, "Are you stupid? Now we're both down here."

The friend says, "Yeah, but I've been down here before and I know the way out."

~Aaron Sorkin

I've Been There

"He's in a heightened panic most of the day and can't go to work," says Beth, a fellow counselor, reporting on a client during our weekly meetings. The familiar dread brews in my belly. "His wife can't talk to him about anything. He's having trouble making plans or decisions. He habitually picks the skin on his nose. He's lost forty pounds and the medicine isn't helping him."

This is the third case presentation I'm listening to and sweat tingles under my arms. I look at the other faces around the table, searching for something to keep me in the here and now before my anxious mind throws me into a confusion of rapid thoughts. My efforts to calm myself turn against me.

Everyone looks fine. They are so lucky!

Working as a social worker in an outpatient psychiatric clinic, my team meets regularly with the psychiatrist to consult on our most difficult cases. Lately, during these meetings I've been having this odd sensation that starts at my skin and crawls straight to my heart.

I'm worse, I think. *My anxiety is worse than every person they are talking about. I'm supposed to be the person who helps others, but I'm helpless to stop what's going on in my own mind.*

I become hyperaware of the room — the tapping pen across the table, the smell of the coffee on the table, the back of my coworker's head as he nods at the doctor's advice — these are all beacons for my attention.

Then, suddenly the room blurs out of focus. Blinking, I look down at the table. *Hold yourself together!* Tears threaten. *I'm falling apart.* My heart rate increases and the walls of the room start to close in.

How am I going to handle life like this?

Unable to sit in that conference room another minute, I awkwardly rise from the table and walk out with my head down. Shame reddens my face as I'm certain all eyes are on my back, judging what a mess I am. *Why is she suddenly leaving in the middle of a meeting?*

And then I'm out the door, making for the stairwell. When I get there, I begin running toward the exit. This happens sometimes when I'm anxious. I feel the desire to run away. As if I could ever *outrun* anxiety.

But this time was different. I couldn't live like this any longer. This time I'd had it with anxiety traps. On this day, leaving that meeting, blowing down the stairs and bolting out the door, I wasn't running away. I was running *toward* something.

I was running toward feeling better.

I was so desperate to feel better that I was willing to do whatever it would take to free myself from living with this kind of suffering. Life didn't feel precious in that moment. It felt hard. It felt unbearable.

It felt like I was losing my mind, my identity and my spirit to anxiety. But somehow I knew that I was still in there somewhere, and I couldn't let it take me over completely. I *would* not! I needed to get my freedom back from anxiety's stranglehold.

Anxiety was not going to win my life. I was determined that day to find out what I needed to stop anxiety, committing myself to practicing it with my heart and soul. That vow was the turning point for me. I got myself out of the hole.

I'll jump in *your* hole and show you the way out, too.

Cowards die many times before their deaths;
the valiant never taste of death but once.
~Caesar, in *Julius Caesar*

Anxiety was first recruited into my life when I was just five years old.

It was February 1977. We tumbled out of our wood-paneled station wagon, returning home from "Indian Princesses," a YMCA craft and activity program to enhance relationships between fathers and daughters.

I was as carefree as they come. My world was interesting and fun. Giggling and poking my sister, I was oblivious to the way the constructs of mortality would soon become clear, falling on me like a ton of bricks.

During that evening's session we learned about Abraham Lincoln and George Washington.

As we climbed the front steps, I asked, "Where are the presidents now, Daddy?"

If I had known that the answer would have such an impact, that my perception of life would so drastically change, I imagine that I wouldn't have been so nonchalant.

There was snow on the ground, ice on the driveway, a smile on our faces. I still feel sad remembering the loss of innocence about to happen. And here it comes, like a cloud covering the sun.

"They're dead," my father said.

"What's dead?" I asked in a singsong voice.

He winced. Uh-oh. It meant my father was uncomfortable with this topic. He comes from a large family of Italian-Americans who suffered an excessive fear of illness and death.

He panicked. He looked at me wondering how he could possibly answer this bright-eyed, rosy-cheeked soul without crushing me.

He tried to answer casually, but I read the panic in his eyes. He tilted his head and changed his voice to a strained whisper. I realized *dead* was definitely bad news.

"It means you're not alive anymore."

Gulp!

"It's like sleeping without waking up. We all die."

What? Mid-skip, I stopped in my tracks. My stomach dropped and my eyes opened wide as if for the first time. Alarms went off in my head.

My smile evaporated, hope vanished and joy disappeared. *Dead was bad.*

"Bad" of this magnitude didn't exist until this point. And now that *bad* existed, fear of *bad* was brought to life like Frankenstein's monster with the lightning bolt. A context was created for fear to settle into.

And settle in it did. I felt the betrayal go straight to my heart, shattering my assumption that life was singularly happy. Introductions were made — Jodi, meet fear. Fear, meet Jodi.

I'm not happy to meet you.

My world was now a place where "the worst" could happen. Tears filled my eyes and I heaved loud sobs as I grieved the happy girl I was before this harrowing revelation. She was lost.

Hearing the wailing even before she met us at the door, my mother tried to assess what had happened. She looked from my sister, who shrugged, to my father's confused expression, then to me lying on the floor of the foyer, weeping uncontrollably.

I was never the same. Time became my enemy as I assumed the seconds, minutes and hours would fill with anxiety and become unmanageable. As fear and anxiety took root in my life, the ability to eat, sleep, or be alone was seriously challenged.

Considering fearful events such as when "my time" would come and when my family might "leave me" was a constant obsession. For a few months I made my mother read to me to get my mind off of it. At the end of each book, the thoughts and images would return immediately, sending me into another panic. I would grab her arm, cry and tighten my body into a ball. She'd rush to start another book to bring me back.

The most horrible visions of decomposing flesh, ghosts and ghouls ran through my mind. I feared the death or illness of a loved one. It was like I was virtually experiencing death, over and over, countless times for the next twenty years.

I would be okay for weeks or months at a time over those two decades, but anxiety was present more than it was ever absent. During the more intense periods, anxiety ran my life. In third grade I had such frequent nervous belly aches that my parents took me to the pediatrician. I'd lost a third of my body weight and I was diagnosed with abdominal migraines. As a teenager, I was severely depressed. As a young adult, I left events early or didn't go, slept with the light on, rarely expressed how I felt and struggled with my weight and self-esteem.

I Got Out

I'll share many more stories of my anxiety in other chapters, but for now I'll fast-forward those twenty years. You want to know how I got better, right?

The last intense anxiety period went on for seven months when I was thirty-one years old. I found myself in those weekly psychiatric consultation meetings comparing myself to all of our "hardest to help" clients. On the day I walked out of that room, fled down the stairs and escaped from the building, I ran out on anxiety trying to cripple me. It was *that* day I committed myself to being proactive and really understanding anxiety, so I could get rid of it.

I began my journey by trying everything. I tried mindfulness, yoga, eating better, deep breathing, Ayurveda, distraction, energy work, exercise, *A Course in Miracles,*[2] medication, herbs, isolation, Bach flowers, acupuncture, NAET,[3] avoidance and so much more.

---

2 *A Course in Miracles.* Temecula, CA: Foundation for Inner Peace, 2007. See acim.org

I appreciated all of them for different reasons. I stayed up all night becoming enlightened about the history of other cultures and my own. I honed clean eating habits, found out the secret life of plants, developed my own unique spirituality, encouraged my creativity, began daily brain healing practices, discovered deep breathing, took long walks in the woods, learned about myself and began to embrace self-love. These changed my life in many ways. They calmed me down, and decreased the episodes of panic. But they didn't change the deeply seeded fear still in my heart — the thought, *Can I handle life?*

It was a change in belief that finally turned these feelings around. With the help of the ideas of Narrative Therapy[4] — the modality I use in conversations with my clients — I finally learned how to stop anxiety in its tracks.

These are three tenets that came into my awareness to make that happen.

- Accept that I deserve to feel better.
- Recognize the tricks that anxiety uses to affect me the way it does.
- Connect with my agency.

Accept that you deserve to feel better.

This idea came to me like many such ideas come to us — from a loved one. This time it was my husband, Ted, who brought it to my attention.

In the midst of my worst panic period, when I was just a shadow of myself, Ted asked, "Why don't you ask Jesus to help?"

This never dawned on me before. My faith primarily prompted me into helping others who were suffering. Asking Jesus to help

---

3   Nambudripad's Allergy Elimination Techniques. See naet.com
4   See Maps of Narrative Practice by Michael White

me when I wasn't suffering as badly as most people in the world seemed ludicrous. I told him so.

"But," said Ted, "You *are* suffering."

The truth of this stunned me. Because I wasn't living in a war zone, an abusive relationship, a natural disaster, abject poverty or afflicted with a terminal illness, I didn't think of what I was going through as *suffering*.

I'd learned about "deserving poor" and "undeserving poor" in social work school — the categories our culture puts on our most vulnerable populations. We were taught to challenge this archaic notion that we are authorities on whether some people deserve help and others don't. But nowhere was I expected to turn this understanding inward or to be kind to myself.

Without being aware of it, I considered myself as undeserving and unworthy of help. My sense of worth was getting in the way of my recovery from anxiety. And as I started to explore this, I realized how large a barrier it could be.

We all have obstacles in our lives, literal and metaphorical, and there isn't a heck of a lot we can do about them when we don't even know they exist. It's only when we see them that we can begin to problem-solve our way around these obstacles. I knew I had a huge wall of anxiety blocking my
path, but I didn't know about the gigantic framework of low self-esteem holding that wall in place.

There was a time I had a plantar wart on the bottom of my left foot. When the pain got to the point that I couldn't walk normally, I went to the dermatologist to get it burned off. I went every month for seven months with no change. The wart was so sore that I walked differently, causing my knees to swell and my hips to become inflamed. This whole time, I didn't think of myself as sick and needing to heal. I always spoke about how lucky I was to be healthy.

I mean, a wart doesn't count, right?

Then, it dawned on me. This was a question of deserving. Since I "wasn't sick" I didn't deserve sympathy for my pain, I didn't deserve help around the house while I healed, nor did I deserve to stop doing everything for everyone else so I could focus on getting myself better. If I didn't deserve to heal, did that mean I deserved to have the wart?

This was crazy! I sat down in meditation and asked my wart what it was trying to tell me. It told me that I walked around all day serving everybody else — but I had to take care of myself, too. The wart was trying to get me to stop being everybody's maid, waitress, nurse, teacher and office manager by making it too painful to walk.

I was so ready to get rid of the wart that I listened. I told the wart I was committed to taking care of myself, so it didn't have to worry. I stuck to that commitment by delegating chores, making plans with girlfriends and going to bed earlier. The wart was completely gone in two weeks.

The first step in addressing this "not-deserving wall" was to show myself some compassion — to give myself some understanding for the pain and suffering I experienced. This meant that instead of judging myself for being weak and stupid, I could acknowledge myself by saying, "I get it."

What an incredible relief this was to my psyche! Saying, "I get it," changes the game. We're validated and can lay down the cross (the "negative self-judgment") and rest. Then, we can get up and — with that more loving relationship with ourselves — start to get better faster.

Ted's question opened up this new understanding, and I realized that suffering was suffering. No one, not even me, deserved to suffer. And everyone, even me, deserved help to get rid of it. So I practiced being easier on myself, stopped beating myself up about my anxiety, and I asked Jesus for help.[5] This self-compassion helped me to like and trust myself and begin to see glimpses of the good skills I used to cope with life. Quickly, I felt less vulnerable and more empowered to make the change I so desired — to get better.

Recognize the tricks and tactics anxiety uses to get power.

Next, I made it my job to learn what this anxiety business was and how it worked — most important, how it worked on me. I was curious to know what was happening in my brain and how it affected my abilities. How does anxiety influence me? What tack did it take? Where did it get its power? What did it need from me to work? How did it get me to agree to its lies?

Breaking down anxiety by asking these questions was a major life-changer for me.[6] When people experience problems, they all too often think of themselves as that problem. "I am fat." "I am stupid." "I am anxious." The problem becomes part of their identity and damages their self-image, compounding their poor experience. In Narrative Therapy the problem is seen as outside the person, so instead of thinking you *are* anxiety, you recognize that you're a person who has *a relationship with* anxiety. Performing an exposé on anxiety, as you're doing when you ask these questions, helps you understand anxiety on every level. The better you understand it, the more equipped you are to respond when it tries to influence you.

In this way, anxiety is seen as a separate entity.

In my own recovery and in thousands of conversations I've had during my twenty years as a therapist, I discovered fifteen

---

5   You don't have to be spiritual to get over anxiety, I share this here to be open and honest about my story. You can talk to a friend, a family member, the Universe, Angels, God, Mohamed, Buddha, or the highest wisdom within you.
6   These questions were inspired by Michael White.

common tricks and tactics that anxiety employs on people to exercise its power. At first, people don't know that these are tricks. Anxiety has us convinced they are very scary truths. Anxiety says, "Something bad will happen," and if you think this is truth, it can really freak you out. But when you know it's a trick, you have the advantage.

It's exactly like a sports team scouting out the competition. You watch their games to learn their moves and know the players' strengths and weaknesses. This gives you an advantage when you're strategizing for the next contest.

When you discover the characteristics of anxiety, you know how to plan ahead and which skills will lead you to faster recovery.

By doing an exposé on anxiety for myself, I learned the main ways anxiety scared the pants off me. It told me I had no future. It immobilized me and scared me. It isolated me. And it aligned itself with concepts that are truly frightening (death, terminal illness, war).

In my suffering, *serving* anxiety became my top priority, because nothing else mattered except trying to relieve it. I thought that satisfying anxiety was the only way to survive it, but I was feeding it power over my life. While I was under its spell, I didn't take risks and skipped doing things I enjoyed to avoid feeling anxious. That's exactly what anxiety wanted me to do. I didn't realize that in the effort to feel better, I was making the anxiety worse by staying home with nothing to distract me from the scary world outside.

When I realized anxiety was not me, and I was not anxiety, I could see the differences in what we wanted. Anxiety wanted me to stay alone and scared so I would stay vulnerable. I wanted to feel happy. Soon, I was able to start calling anxiety out on the lies it was telling me. Its power quickly deflated.

Connect with your agency.

At this same time, Narrative Therapy taught me how to connect with my personal agency. I learned that we are each of us agents of our lives, meaning we affect and create our lives through our choices and responses. Of course, unexpected things happen to us in life, but we don't have to be a passive recipient of those things. We have agency (power) to respond to them, and we get to choose exactly how, what, when and where we respond.

This is the cool thing. This response makes or breaks our lives much more than what happened. So while the things that happen to us may be out of our control — they might be awful, terrorizing, traumatizing or unjust — our response to them is fully, completely, utterly under our control. It's that very response — the way we think about what happened, the actions we took during and after, how we express what is important to us, how we make meaning around that event — that rules our mood, health and contentment, our sense of self and our relationships. Ultimately this response defines how we remember the experience and relive it throughout our lives.

Up until learning this, I thought anxiety came and went of its own will. I had no sense of how *I made it* come and go. I've seen this same lack of awareness in many of my clients, so I understand it's a pretty typical phenomenon. The more people are disconnected or unaware of their personal agency, the less happy they are with their lives. Happiness is not a given in life. Happy people generate that happiness. Feeling vulnerable and susceptible makes you feel powerless. When people believe they have no power, they feel unlucky, unworthy and different from everyone else, adding to their fear and despair. They can't figure out how to generate happiness. This is how I felt, too.

Once, I was on a business trip. Being away and alone was a trigger for my anxiety. While I was gone, my grandfather was scheduled for an emergency open heart surgery. Surgery —

anything life or death related — was another trigger for me. I remember being in bed — nighttime was *also* a trigger for me — feeling anxious with my mind and my heart racing. I could feel the energy under my skin as if I would pop open any minute. Due to old habits, my first inclination was to try outrunning anxiety in my mind. But knowing I was scared, anxiety ran after me, terrorizing me with its threats. *You can't handle this. You're going to freak out right now. You are about to go out of your mind. You can't stop it.*

I was cowering in my bed with my hands over my ears.

Then, remembering Narrative Therapy, I began to coach myself through. At first, I couldn't figure out how to have personal agency in a situation when I was a world away and powerless to do anything to help my grandfather. So I decided to pray.

At first it was a passive prayer. In a passive prayer, you feel like a victim of the world begging for mercy. You feel unable to change anything, and an act of God is the only hope.

Frederick Douglass once said, "I prayed for twenty years and received no answer until I started praying with my legs."

When I remembered that quote, I changed to *active* praying by sending good intentions to my grandfather during his surgery. I emailed home offering as much support as I could from the distance. Then, I arranged a friend to deliver meals to my grandmother. Now I could see myself as a *helper* rather than a *helpless* beggar.

Actively praying isn't unusual. What made a difference to me during this panic was simply that I recognized it as an action and felt powerful, instead of powerless. Just feeling powerful made my anxiety go down. I didn't have to lie in my bed feeling vulnerable and waiting for something bad to happen. I could affect the situation.

Anxiety did not take over that evening. It was the first of many times I consciously turned to my agency — the power to respond, act or contribute to the situation — which averted the panic attack threatening to ruin my night.

The more anxious people are, the less they feel connected to their skills or even feel that they have agency in their life. Even extremely anxious people are taking some kind of action, but if they don't perceive it as in their control, like Donna through her husband's emergency, they'll still feel out of control.

> *God, give me grace to accept with serenity*
> *the things that cannot be changed,*
> *Courage to change the things*
> *which should be changed,*
> *and the Wisdom to distinguish*
> *the one from the other.*
> ~Reinhold Niebuhr

This *Serenity Prayer* is a mantra for millions of people's healing. The important part is that last line. When I began to focus on the power and wisdom that I had, instead of lamenting what was out of my control, I became an active participant in my life and *that* changed the game.

It was an advantage I never knew I had. Knowing I *could* do something allowed me to knock anxiety out of the park.

On social media we read of all the gurus telling us that we have a choice to be happy. Without them explaining *how* to be happy, this does little good and can do some damage. It makes people like you and me who feel like we've tried everything and would try anything to feel better — and still don't feel happy — judge ourselves to be an utter failure.

When you're depressed and trying to feel better, "You have a choice," doesn't make sense, which can be more unsettling than the depression. Your mind seeks answers and as you search for understanding, you often figure either you're not doing it right or there's a reason you are supposed to feel bad, like, you're being punished for something.

For so long during the years of my anxiety and depression, hearing that advice — that I had a choice — invalidated my efforts to survive and supported the idea that I was undeserving. It invited horribly negative self-judgment and increased my suffering. It made me want to punch someone in the face. I felt misunderstood and judged by those claims that all I had to do to feel better was to *choose it*.

I wanted to scream, "You don't understand!"

And yet, at the same time, a doubting voice inside said, "It's probably you who don't understand, Jodi. You don't get anything right."

I was stuck in this conflict for a long time. Defending myself. Blaming myself. My mind trying to make sense, but perpetually confusing itself. This was such a source of suffering.

It was only when I had compassion for myself and became more loving toward myself and my problems that I could finally accept how I had agency — or power — to feel better without enticing self-judgment. And this was so much easier now that I'd broken down anxiety's power by exposing the lies it told me to keep me vulnerable. And once I accepted that I had personal power, I could connect to my power in ways that I couldn't before.

For me, all three of these tenets helped me move past anxiety.

- I had to believe that I deserved to feel better and let go of negative self-judgment.
- I had to recognize the tricks that anxiety used to affect me the way it does, so I could see that anxiety was a big fat liar.
- I had to learn how to connect with my personal agency so I could find and trust the power that I have.

That's how I recovered, and now I'm going to show you how.

These ideas are tried and true, tested on myself and thousands of others. They work because they strategically target anxiety at the roots.

It's time to explain fear, break it down into its smaller components and make you feel better about yourself so that you can get over your anxiety once and for all.

History of a Bully

It takes a lot less work to feel good than it does to feel bad.
~Alan Cohen

I've always found it extremely helpful when I have a problem to understand what I'm up against. I'm also a science nerd who finds this very interesting. When I show people how problems get out of hand, they see a way forward. When I teach people the biological, cultural, mental and relational history of fear and anxiety, a light bulb goes off and a weight is lifted from their shoulders. They stop blaming themselves.

The more you feel like you understand something, the more you feel in control. That feeling of control is the key to getting rid of anxiety in your life.

How Anxiety Gets Out of Hand

Lots of things happen to us in our life and they set off emotional responses. This is human. For example, you might feel "Loss" if someone breaks up with you. (See the black circle in Figure 1 that represents the amount of sorrow you feel.)

This is devastating enough. But it doesn't stop there. Next, you compound it by negatively judging your response. *Am I overreacting? Why can't I keep a relationship? How could I mess this up? Why does everyone leave me?* (The grey dotted circles in Figure 1 represent the amount of unhappiness you feel from each of these thoughts.)

And then, fear sets in when you worry about how you can't handle feeling this bad over any amount of time. Especially if you see yourself as someone with "no skills." *How am I going to do this? How long is this going to last? I can't do this! OMG! OMG! I'm losing my mind!* (The striped circles in Figure 1 represent the amount of worry you feel from each of these fears.)

Figure 1.

Black: Original feeling: "Loss"
Grey dotted: Negative self-judgments
Striped: Fears and anxieties

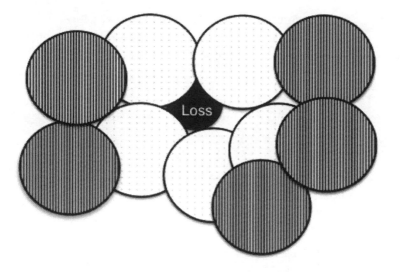

Note that the combination of the dotted and striped circles is greater than the size of the black circle alone. The intensity of emotions has gone from the original small sorrow of loss "A" to the size of the entire misery of "B" with the negative self-judgments and fear. (See Figure 2.)

Figure 2.

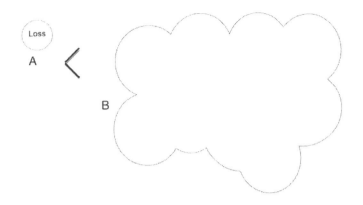

Usually you don't realize each of these separate steps. It feels like a single reaction and it's overwhelming. Often you end up negatively judging yourself again on top of it all, adding insult to injury: *Why do I take things so personally? Why am I not over this by now? My ex doesn't seem to be this upset. I'm so weak.* The overwhelmed feeling expands. (Black dotted circles in Figure 3.)

Figure 3.

Black dotted: Secondary layer of negative self-judgments

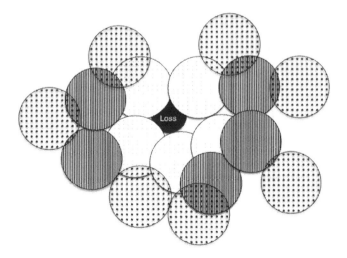

This passionate beating up of yourself is so stressful. It makes you not trust yourself and continues to trigger a biological response in your body. It exponentially intensifies our emotions and, because they keep you stuck in shame and guilt, the healing process is lengthened.

Biology of Fear

Fear doesn't shut you down; it wakes you up.
~Veronica Roth, *Divergent*

Fear affects everyone and everything, human *and* animal. It has a cognitive purpose, leading us to read situations, to reason and act in ways that lower our risk for harm, such as looking both ways before crossing the street, eating our vegetables and buckling up.

More importantly, fear has a biological purpose. When physical danger is present — a stressful situation — your brain sends a signal to the adrenal glands to produce the hormones cortisol, adrenaline and noradrenaline. They fill you with energy, preparing your body to perform beyond your usual limits in order to fight off or run away from the danger. Think of the ancient caveman being surprised by the hungry saber-tooth tiger in the woods. The sympathetic nervous system is triggered by this dangerous situation, giving the caveman energy to attempt survival by fighting or fleeing.

When confronted with danger, your amygdala, which is an almond-shaped cluster in the temporal lobe of your brain (See Figure 4.), recognizes the trigger and signals the release of the hormones.[7] These hormones prepare your muscles and senses to

---

7   A. Jansen, X. Nguyen, V. Karpitsky, and M. Mettenleiter, "Central Command Neurons of the Sympathetic Nervous System: Basis of the Fight-or-Flight Response," *Science Magazine* 5236 (27 October 1995): 270.

take strong physical action and be mentally attentive enough to think on your feet.

Figure 4.

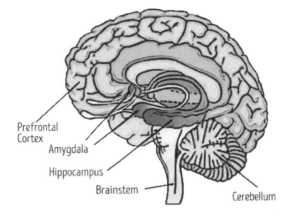

They set in motion a whole series of physiological reactions in your body such as faster breathing (to bring oxygen to large muscle groups), a rapid heart rate (to pump that oxygen to those large muscles), restricted blood vessels for digestion (to save the blood for large muscle groups), dilated blood vessels for your muscles (which would allow you to run or defend yourself), dilated pupils, tunnel vision and even an increase in body heat (because warm muscles perform better).

The body's response to danger happens so incredibly fast. The amygdala doesn't decide if something is dangerous. It is elicited by *emotional memories*, so it responds immediately when it recognizes a familiar sight, smell or sound it associates with danger. It can be a past or genetic memory. Genetic memory refers to memory associated with instinct. There are some things your instinct remembers as dangerous even if you've never experienced them before.[8]

---

8   Brian Dias and Kerry Ressler, "Parental olfactory experience influences behavior and neural structure in subsequent generations," *Nature Neuroscience* 17 (2014): 89–96

The sympathetic nervous system response happens before reasoning can take place. This is because cognitive reasoning takes time and when in danger, the body can't spare the time. It needs to be ready. The amygdala stores fear memories or, more specifically, the emotions of fear rather than a cognitive memory. Emotional response is faster than cognitive response. This is so the reaction to danger can happen as quickly as possible.[9]

While the amygdala signals your body to get ready, it also sends a signal to the cortex, another part of the brain just behind your forehead, where cognitive reasoning takes place. The cortex analyzes the fear stimulus in detail using information from many different parts of the brain to see if you're *really* facing a threat. If it is a threat, the body is already prepared to take action.

This next part is crucial for you to understand so that you can stop beating yourself up about your anxiety.

When your cortex decides you're in danger, it has your body begin actions in self-preservation. Your focus is on the tasks at hand and worry gets relegated to the background. Fear is dismissed and deemed unnecessary. It did its job. Action helps you feel empowered in the moment. When the danger passes, you've used up all of the sympathetic nervous system energy and feel gratitude and pride that you survived. When you're not in danger, the cortex sends a message back to the amygdala saying, "Everything is okay. Cut the hormones!" but there's nothing to do with the adrenaline coursing through your body that will take some time to go away. For example, if your roommate startles you somehow, your sympathetic nervous system responds. Your heart rate increases, you'll feel a rush in your body and your breathing will change. You

---

9   JN Perusini, EM Meyer, VA Long, V Rau, N Nocera, J Avershal, J Maksymetz, I Spigelman, and MS Fanselow, "Induction and Expression of Fear Sensitization Caused by Acute Traumatic Stress," *Neuropsychopharmacology* (6 August 2015): 45–57

may even yell out. When you realize that you're okay, you'll feel your body still *zing* for the next ten minutes or so until it settles.

If your sympathetic nervous system was triggered by a sound *similar* to a past danger (perhaps a tire blowing out sounding like a gunshot, or the voice of an abuser), the biological response can be scary and uncomfortable. Even though you're not in physical danger, the panic *feels* dangerous, and this causes the cortex to *think* there's a real risk so it sustains the stress hormones. Your body instinctively wants to act, but there's nothing to do. A feeling of helplessness arises which increases the emotions. This useless, horrible feeling is what I call anxiety. Even though your rational mind knows you're physically safe, anxiety and panic ensues.

Here's why. Your neurons, the little brain cells that take the message from the amygdala to the cortex, are highly developed. This is evolution at its finest, since being quick at responding to keep ourselves safe is an essential characteristic to ensure survival. However, the neurons that take the message from the cortex back to the amygdala are less developed. This means that triggering a fear response is automatic, but turning it off gets a bit tricky. It's far easier to trigger a fear response than to turn it off.

In an article in the December 14, 2007 *Newsweek*, entitled "The Roots of Fear," Sharon Begley writes:

The evolutionary primacy of the brain's fear circuitry makes it more powerful than the brain's reasoning faculties. The amygdale sprouts a profusion of connections to higher brain regions—neurons that carry one-way traffic from the amygdale to neocortex. Few connections run from the cortex to the amygdale, however. That allows the amygdale to override the products of the logical, thoughtful cortex, but not vice-versa. So although it is sometimes possible to think yourself out of fear ("I know that dark shape in the alley is a garbage can"), it takes great effort and persistence. Instead, fear tends to overrule reason, as the amygdale hobbles our logic and reasoning circuits. That makes fear "far more powerful than reason," says neurobiologist Michael Fanselow of the University of California, Los Angeles. "It evolved as a mechanism to protect us from life threatening situations, and from an evolutionary standpoint, there is nothing more import-ant than that."

Anxiety is not your fault! It's biological.

Fear is an emotional response that triggers the brain to keep us alive. It is your friend. But because the turn-off valve is not so automatic, it's important for you to do some of the heavy lifting.

When you're anxious, but clearly not in physical danger, you need to override the amygdala consciously by worrying less about how your body is feeling and by distracting yourself until your body calms down on its own.

Taking action can help.

A 2010 study published in *Neuron* with scientists in Italy at the European Molecular Biology Laboratory (EMBL)[10] looked at this very idea of actively participating in the fear response. In the study, lab mice took an active or passive response to fear. In the mice that took a passive response, the researchers triggered a specific neuron and the mice switched to an active response.

The study found that the change from a passive to an active fear response was accompanied by the activation of large parts of the cortex. Once the mice were active, their cortex signaled the release of gamma-aminobutyric acid (GABA) to put the brakes on the cortisol and adrenaline which means the action improved the work of those less-developed neurons from the amygdala to the cortex.

---

10   Alessandro Gozzi et al., "A Neural Switch for Active and Passive Fear," Neu-ron 67, no. 4 (26 August 2010): 656-666.

Action helps us decrease anxiety! Action releases GABA that stops the adrenal glands from continuing to release panic-inducing hormones. Now, I don't like my anxiety, I never did. So knowing that *taking action helps* is all the information I need to motivate me to move my body and mind. I'd move mountains to stop this feeling.

Tom

I met with Tom, a college student who had very little confidence even though he was very smart. He told me that he sat in his chair in his dorm room for hours, physically and mentally immobilized by anxiety about his perception of himself as a failure. The more he stayed still, the harder it was for him to do anything. He began skipping classes and avoiding work, ending the semester with unfinished assignments in three classes, risking his scholarship.

This was when his parents brought him to me, really worried about his future. Tom explained that whenever he sat down to do homework and came upon something he didn't understand, he felt overwhelmed. He thought, *I can't do this,* and that was that. So he sat in the chair for hours doing nothing.

This happens a lot. Anxiety urges people to make premature and definitive conclusions about their future, so they're trapped in hopelessness. These conclusions seem so true, they exhaust and devastate, preventing people from taking action. This is exactly what anxiety wants.

These are premature conclusions people often make.
"That won't work."
"I won't be able to." "I'll never get a good job."
"Nobody will marry me."
Crushed by the imminent failure, they have no energy or motivation to make any effort toward their dreams. They forget that this assumption is not a truth about their future. If you challenge them, they'll stoutly defend themselves, giving you evidence why it's

true, forgetting that originally it was just a worry that had crossed their mind.

With Tom, I undermined that truth by asking more about it.

"Tom, I'm just curious. Out of the whole assignment, about how much do you struggle with?"

"About five percent."

"Really? And the other ninety-five percent? That's easier?"

"Oh yeah, I can usually do that, no problem."

"But when you come to something you don't know, you stop working?"

"Yes."

"Okay, so you can do about ninety-five percent of the work and if you did that portion, you'd feel okay, but when you come to something you don't know, you forget that you can do most of it and get scared you can't do any of it and stay still for hours? Do I have that right?"

A sheepish grin came across his face as the ridiculousness of the situation was dropped into his brain. My observation, because it came from curiosity, not judgment, allowed his mind some distance to view his situation anew. It was like he'd been too close to it to see anything except his very thin conclusions that *he couldn't do it.*

I told him about the mice and how his sitting made anxiety worse. I asked what would happen if he skipped what he didn't know and finished everything he *did* know, before going back to the harder questions. We wrote down several possibilities.

- He would complete his work and get high grades.
- The rest of the assignment might give him clues about how to do the hard parts.
- If he felt overwhelmed while doing homework, taking a short walk would clear his mind and get him back to work faster than sitting in the chair for hours.
- He'd change the way he saw himself.

After this one conversation where he made a plan to take action instead of staying still, Tom strengthened his neurons and increased his GABA — essentially stopping anxiety. That summer he had great success, completing his assignments ahead of the extension due date and performing well in his internship at a prestigious corporation.

Actions can be widely defined. They can be active, such as taking a walk, repairing something, being creative, cleaning, organizing or working. Or they can be thought changes — believing that you're okay, making decisions, committing to something or learning new information. All of it increases GABA and decreases anxiety.

Because action counters the helplessness that fuels anxiety, it also helps you emotionally recover from anxious thoughts. Doing something has you feeling empowered, reminding you that you've got control over your response.

Culture of Anxiety

Doesn't it seem like everyone has anxiety? That's because they do. It's an epidemic. The Anxiety and Depression Association of America estimate about forty million Americans over eighteen years old experience an anxiety disorder, making it one of the most common mental disorders in the US.[11]

The world is changing fast and everything is speeding up. There is more pressure and more "to do" that fills the day. You're getting less sleep and taking stimulants like caffeine to get more done. Then, you spend your day with high cortisol levels.

In modern culture, stressors and worries stimulate the sympathetic nervous system's responses. Your anxieties are usually about things you feel helpless about like war, climate change, getting sick, violence, a loved one dying or not being good enough. The sense of helplessness feeds and defines the anxiety. You can be

---

11   Find these references on jodiaman.com/you1anxiety0

crippled by it. Your body and brain don't know what to do with the energy they manufacture for action. You have a *burst* of energy and nothing to do with it.

The "fight or flight" system was designed to be a once-in-a-while occurrence, like an encounter with a hungry tiger, not as an everyday, all-day occurrence. The continuous fear responses take a toll on your body, heart and soul, which leads to feeling even more vulnerable and stressed out.

You judge yourself very much for being anxious, but you're ignoring that culture nuances and expectations fuel anxiety. Here are four reasons anxiety is so rampant in our culture. Understanding these will help you be easier on yourself.

1. Physical and emotional

The first reason is your brain's response to toxins, trauma and illness. If you're injured or have a history of trauma or loss, it can cause anxiety to develop. Dr. Daniel Amen, a psychiatrist researching SPECT[12] brain imaging, has shown how these histories affect our brain functioning in many areas directly linked to our emotional experiences.

The violence, poverty and injustice in our culture create an environment for trauma to occur and continue affecting us individually and relationally. Fortunately, Dr. Amen's research illustrates that our brains can and do heal with proper treatment. The process I suggest for healing anxiety will help heal the brain, too.

Some medical problems such as hyperthyroidism, diabetes, PMS, medication side effects, irritable bowel syndrome, heart disease, asthma, drug withdrawal and more are known to increase anxiety.

---

12   SPECT stands for single-photon emission computed tomography, a nuclear imaging test, using radioactive substance and a special camera to create 3-D pictures. While imaging tests like X-rays can show what the structures inside your body look like, a SPECT scan produces images that show how your organs work.

2. Commercialism

The second reason is commercialism. Surprised? This sounds weird, but in the twenty years I've been working with people, I've seen and understood this to be a serious culprit in the increase of anxiety in our culture.

You're constantly bombarded with commercials containing the subliminal message that you deserve their product just for being you. Companies do this to separate you (a potential customer) from your old work-ethic mentality, so you make a quick purchase. When you believe that you have to work for what you want, your buying habits are much more conservative.

Unfortunately, believing you deserve what you want simply because "you are you" embeds a sense of entitlement, which can cause many problems, including anxiety. People begin to expect and believe they should get what they want. And when they can't —for example, if they can't afford it or miss an opportunity — it feels unjust. Confused, our mind begins to question this. We conclude that the reason we can't have what we want is that we must not be worthy of it. This is the easiest explanation we come up with. We feel totally powerless to do something about "not getting something because we're unworthy," because we don't really know *why* we're not worthy.

Confused again, our minds start to search for explanations for why we're unworthy, and we begin listing our inadequacies to make sense of it. Feeling inadequate makes us feel out of control and feeds anxiety.

We've emotionally forgotten our empowered roots. Capitalism is destroying the main tenet of itself — work hard for what you want — to sustain itself and sell products.

It is easy to see how commercialism is affecting us by observing our children. When kids ask for something and we have to say no, the emotional response often feels to us like an over-the-top reaction. They yell, scream, criticize us and have a tantrum. Kids aren't just feeling the loss of the toy they wanted, they are feeling *rejected as a person.*

If we say yes to a request — "I HAVE to have it, Mommy, pleeeeease!" — we're later confused to find it discarded in the back of their closet the next week. Their retail-therapy-high didn't last long. Self-confidence is not sustained by things, especially when we come by them passively. Unless the purchase has some sustaining function of fun, entertainment or helpfulness, it has little value post-checkout. This induces another mini-disappointment, causing children to desire more stuff to compensate.

When kids aren't learning that *taking action* is how to achieve what they desire, they become more passive in their approach to life. The helplessness brings on depression and despair as they decide not to try anything in order to ward off more disappointment. This passivity is the opposite of how to live to be happy.

However, if kids have to earn what they desire, finally obtaining that product symbolizes the work they put in, highlighting their skills and abilities. They see the power to affect their life and surroundings. They understand they can make things happen even through a challenge. They build trust in themselves that they can problem-solve, making them feel less vulnerable to the unpredictable world. Anxiety has no power inside this self-assured attitude.

3. Virtual trauma

The third reason anxiety is so rampant is the constant virtual exposure to trauma.[13] You have ready access on your TV, your smartphone and other electronic devices to images of war and other awful things happening far away.

---

13   R.J. McNally and N. Breslau, "Does virtual trauma cause post-traumatic stress disorder?" *American Psychologist* 63, no. 4 (May-June 2008): 282-3.

A few hundred years ago, if you had a fear trigger, you were present in the experience and could respond. You didn't know about tragedies across the globe.

Now, you're far away from the traumas of the world and there is seemingly nothing you can do from your couch, but watch helplessly. The fear turns into anxiety with this sense of helplessness.

4. People are meaning makers

Anxiety can be recruited into your life in a variety of ways. Usually something happens to make you feel vulnerable. It could be a traumatic experience, such as sexual abuse, war, being mugged or a car accident. Or it could be something else like contracting an illness, having a conflict, experiencing a break-up, being embarrassed or hearing a scary story. Or it may be from something seemingly small. You might simply feel a fear response, because of known or unknown stress, and it feels uncomfortable. Anxiety can start this subtly, but because of the meaning you make around the situation the anxiety can snowball into something quite horrible.

When you experience something, you decide what it means to you. This meaning is highly influenced by your life experiences, your beliefs and your thought habits (e.g., pessimism versus optimism). Anxiety is no exception. The sympathetic nervous system response is only sustained when you're not in physical danger if you *think* you're still vulnerable. When you think you are safe, GABA will shut it off. While the fear response is biological, anxiety is learned and sustained through your meaning-making.

Some people jump out of airplanes or drive motorcycles fast, because they love the thrill of the adrenaline rush. Others feel the same adrenaline rush from emotional stress and then panic, because it feels so unmanageable. How *you* experience this identical feeling depends on the meaning you give it.

You are suffering and I know this only too well. This feeling is real. It's awful. It makes you feel *really* powerless. Anxiety doesn't want you empowered by what I'm saying. It will try to undermine us both by saying what I offer you is impossible or crazy. But I want you to know and feel the power that you have, because that's how you're going to get better. If you know anxiety is learned, you'll realize it can be unlearned.

Meaning of Anxiety *et al.*

So what does anxiety really *mean*?

Many words are used to describe anxiety. Everyone thinks of it and understands it differently. Whatever words you use to illustrate your anxiety come from close to your experience, so go with it. Since I can't ask you what those words are, the following list explains how I'll use certain words in this book.

There may be terms here that you've never associated with anxiety. You'll find it helpful to see examples of how anxiety hides as *other* feelings and problems. Exposing these disguises will give you the advantage.

Fear response is a biological response to dangerous stimuli. It's useful in alerting you to danger and prompting you to keep yourself safe. When you *are* safe, the fear dissipates. You would never want to get rid of fear altogether, since it serves this important function.

Fear, as a noun, is a general term for this emotion and used to categorize other things or concepts you are afraid of. Like, *I have a fear of public speaking.* Or used when speaking generally about the feelings of fear.

Worry is a thought or perception that something is cause for alarm or an anticipation that something bad will happen. You worry about the bad that might happen, if you can't handle a situation. You worry about other people's suffering or that something bad will happen to them.

Nervousness is a slight to moderate physical sensation with or without fearful thoughts. You may still be "handling it" at this point, but you're starting to worry and feel a bit out of your comfort zone. You may be able to push it aside, but you're still fearing that the worst is yet to come. With nervousness, you avoid or opt out of plans or make adjustments to prevent your feelings from intensifying and miss out on experiences you'd otherwise enjoy.

Anxiety is a worry-based physically and emotionally intense sensation due to the release of cortisol and adrenaline hormones that's prompted when you are *not* in physical danger. It may cause gastrointestinal symptoms, rapid breathing and increased heart rate. It's usually accompanied by distressing thoughts as well as a desperation to feel calm again. You feel helpless or worried that you "can't handle it" or that you'll "go crazy." You feel stuck, trapped in a feeling of vulnerability and out of control, even though you're not in immediate danger.

Panic is an amplification of anxiety that includes increased physical sensations and a feeling that you're in imminent danger. (If you were in danger, you'd use that energy to survive. When you're not in danger, it feels overwhelming.) You feel like you want to jump out of your skin, have a need to move your body by pacing or rocking because the cortisol released by your adrenal glands gives you a boost of energy. You feel a sense of desperation for help, *any* help.

Uncomfortable. Many children will use this word to describe their symptoms when they can't relate to the words above. They can relate to feeling uncomfortable even though they don't know why. Any *discomfort* that a person can't describe usually signifies nervousness.

Desperation. The feeling of desperation is a mark of anxiety. It's the urgent desire to be anywhere other than where you are. Desperation confuses you into thinking that anxiety's demands are the ones you need to listen to in order to end your suffering. Such as urgently leave a situation, avoid something, flee — but this often makes the situation worse in the long run.

Out of control. Anxiety has you feeling out of control. That feeling is a trick of anxiety. "Control issues" are anxiety issues. People who have control issues have them because they're afraid something bad might happen if they aren't overseeing and managing things. Being "out of control" feels vulnerable and this freaks us out.

Anger comes from the impatience to escape a feeling that's beyond uncomfortable. It is also used as a power tactic to seek control when one feels like they've lost it. It is extremely common for anxiety to be behind anger.

Stress is like the fear response. I'm using it to describe an overall feeling of exhaustion caused by a pressuring or intense context. Physiologically, it's synonymous with fear, anxiety, and nervousness, because it's caused by the same release of hormones. Stress is socially acceptable, so it's a handy way to describe unwanted feelings without stigma.

Dread convinces you that a bad event is practically inevitable. You expect that "the other shoe will drop." It's a tactic of anxiety and used by the mind as evidence that it *should* be afraid in order to be vigilant when the dreaded thing happens.

OCD is where a person has obsessive thoughts that cause such intense anxiety that he or she engages in compulsive actions to try relieving that anxiety.

Embarrassment is used to describe the worry of what others think. This is often a component in social anxiety. People with social anxiety feel like everyone is looking at them and judging them. You have feelings of inadequacy, incompetency, insufficiency or deficit with embarrassment.

Shyness is instigated by worries. These worries can be varied. For example feeling inferior, worrying about being egotistical, worrying that people will misunderstand or judge you or your opinions as not worthy or wrong. You feel timid or concerned that you might hurt someone or that someone may hurt you.

Phobia is an intense fear of an object or situation that poses little actual danger except in some contexts, but provokes anxiety.

Social anxiety is very common. It's anxiety in social situations usually characterized by worrying about how things will go, how you come across to people, being judged by others and whether or not you'll feel comfortable in public or with a group.

Laziness comes into play when you judge yourself for avoiding things (due to anxiety). You might label yourself as lazy. Some people *are* lazy, of course, but most people lack motivation because they feel defeated by the prospect of doing something with anxiety. It feels challenging to even try when anxiety convinces you there's very little chance of success. Anxious people are not unmotivated, they're *highly motivated* to resist doing what might make them uncomfortable.

Impatience often comes with nervousness or worries. When people are anxious, their mind is filled with the anxious thoughts and feelings and it's hard to deal with anything else.

Overwhelmed is how anxiety makes you feel, because it feels so big and out of control. You feel your emotion is more than what you can handle in that moment. It's not pleasant and feeds itself.

Preoccupied is when worries take up your brain space that you could be using for something else.

I use a lot of these terms interchangeably, because I think of them as the same thing. They all have things in common in the way they affect and disempower people.

Take action

Did I miss one? What name do you give to what you feel? Describe it by writing it down.

_____

_____

_____

_____

_____

_____

_____

_____

Relationship with Anxiety

Better out than in, I always say.

~Shrek

Sometimes anxiety's voice gets internalized and sounds very much like your own voice saying, "Something bad is going to happen." The voice makes anxiety seem true and important, as if it's a skill you've learned to protect yourself. It can become your identity. *I am anxious.*

This is a dirty rotten trick. Anxiety is not you. It never was you. It never will be you. You are a person who has an unfortunate current relationship with anxiety where it influences you, antagonizes you and torments you.

Relationships change.

The easiest way to begin changing your relationship with anxiety is to I decided to jump from it. Using externalizing language such as "the anxiety," even capitalizing it and personifying it ("Why does Anxiety say that?"), is a good start. Naming anxiety is another step in getting your power back. It makes anxiety, which holds power by being evasive, more tangible. Also you can separate yourself from anxiety by "taking a step back."

When you go through emotionally charged events, you're close to the chaos where you're governed by being overwhelmed. Taking a step back brings you out of that chaos where you can see the event from a new perspective. We'll go into this technique further in Chapter Six, so I'll just explain quickly here how I picture getting distance for myself. In my mind's eye, I imagine myself on the side of a mountain observing my current situation being played out below in the valley. It's as if I'm the director of a movie. I see myself and all the people involved below acting like they are acting, and feeling like they are feeling, but from this distance I can see more of a big picture view. Being free from my worry up at this vantage point, I feel empowered. I can read the world and other people better by understanding why they do what they do.

With this understanding, it's easier for me to see my ability to respond in a way that's comfortable for me. Now I can trust in myself. Anxiety loses power and influence over me. Space is freed up in my mind to decide what actions I can take.

Thinking of anxiety as outside of me was pivotal in my healing journey. I invite my clients to get distance as well.

Sheree

Sheree[14] is a wonderfully loving, thoughtful and compassionate woman who knows her people skills which she applies in small groups and one-on-one situations. She describes herself as empathetic — providing what a person needs before they're even aware of it. She rents out apartments and has an impressive sales record. She says she makes people feel at ease and heard, by joking and helping people feel welcome and giving them a sense of belonging.

She calls this self "Work Sheree" and in therapy, confides in me that that it's "not really her." The "Real Sheree" is terrified of everything. She can't drive on the expressway, be in public, make financial decisions, stop worrying about her boys, be alone — the problems go on and on. She describes her anxiety as a disability that's been around for forty years. Even though she would love to get better, her ideas about her anxieties offer her no wiggle room. She "can't" and that's that.

That she's one Sheree at work and another outside of work is an undisputed truth.

In our conversation, I ask questions that invite Sheree to separate her identity from her anxiety by talking about her fears from a distance.

What does Anxiety have you thinking when you are in the grocery store?

What does Anxiety say about what other people are thinking?

What does Anxiety say might happen?

This breaks anxiety down.

---

14   This interview was recorded in a podcast. Search Love Yourself Up with Jodi Aman in iTunes. It's Episode *Interview with Jodi's Client Sheree: How to Handle Anxiety When It Shows Up.* You can find it on the book page: jodiman. com/you1anxiety0

Then, I ask about the Work-Sheree-skills in different everyday scenarios. We quickly discover that there is evidence of Work Sheree *outside* of work — she's kind to her children, she has confidence that people like her one-on-one, she has coping skills to get along in the world, and she understands people in all settings.

This challenges her taken-for-granted assumptions about anxiety that "Real Sheree" is completely disabled. It doesn't take long before she begins to tell me how silly it is to think that Work Sheree isn't *real*, when Work-Sheree-skills are employed in many other contexts.

Reflecting on this, she brightens and says, "She is me and I like that me!"

Sheree stopped identifying with anxiety and decided to practice being Work Sheree (now just Sheree) in everything she does. Anxiety had told her that she *can't*. She thought this was the truth. Once she realized this was just a trick of anxiety, we found a way to connect her with the skills and power she already had, and we began to move forward.

Anxiety doesn't play fair. It is not your friend. It will say whatever it can to get you to believe it. It's full of tactics to torment you. Now that you understand anxiety's background, let's look more closely at the mind of anxiety so you can anticipate its plays and get the ball back in your court as quickly as possible.

Anxiety Playbook

Nothing in life is to be feared. It is only to be understood.
~Marie Curie

Samantha

Through and since all of this, Cindy told me, Samantha remained calm and engaged in life and school. Everything changed in the few weeks before Samantha was brought to me. Cindy explained what anxiety was up to in Samantha's life. Samantha cried and begged to stay home from school every morning. When she finally did go to school, she spent much of the day negotiating with the counselor to call her mother.

Eyeing Samantha as we both listened to her mother, I saw her features start to relax. I wasn't sure, but I wondered if I saw something else, too, as she looked up through her long eyelashes. Something that told me she had done some very serious thinking about this anxiety.

That sparked my curiosity. I engaged Samantha to hear her thoughts on what was happening.

"Samantha, can you tell me why you want to call your mom when you are at school?"

"To make sure she's still alive."
"What does Anxiety tell you is happening to her?"
"I'm afraid that she might be dead."
"How do you imagine she might die?"

Anxiety puts visions in our heads about awful things that could happen. These visions are seen as if they are real. They trigger a sympathetic nervous system response. Since it's my job to break down the power of these images, I ask these questions to understand exactly what they are communicating to Samantha.

Now it's her turn to be curious. These aren't questions anyone has asked her before. Up until now, when she says, "I'm afraid of Mom dying," people simply shake their heads sympathetically. They understand, *Mom had cancer. Cancer is scary. Mom dying is scary.* Everybody can relate. They don't ask questions. And this validates Samantha's anxiety.

I don't do this. I want to keep asking. I'm curious to learn her anxiety's particularities in order to pick it apart and deflate its power over her. I start by externalizing anxiety (separating it from her identity) using my language: "What does Anxiety tell you is happening to your mom while you're at school?" This is instead of, *What do you think will happen to her?*

This portrays the idea that anxiety is a separate entity telling her frightening things. This isn't a technique — it's how I think about anxiety. I'm interested in the exact tricks it uses to take over her life, so that we know how to stop it.

Samantha answers, "I'm worried that she might be kidnapped or get in a car crash, or get cancer again."

"Okay, so you have a worry about her being kidnapped, a worry about her getting into a car crash and a worry about her getting cancer again? What's it like when you feel worried?"

"I can't concentrate, my heart races, I feel overheated. I'm terrified. I just want to go home."

"What's it like when you're home?"

"I'm not scared, because I can see my mom."

"If you can see your mom, she can't be kidnapped, or if you're riding in the car, she can't get in a car crash — and if you're with her, her cancer can't get her?"

Samantha smiles for the first time. I invited her to see her anxiety from a distance. When you're close and feeling it, anxiety is so convincing. Just in this moment of distance — my questions deliberately do this to draw her outside the chaos — she already sees holes in anxiety's arguments.

Anxiety has so many tricks it uses to get us to believe in it. Over the years of talking to people of all ages about their anxieties, I began to see some common ways anxiety worked. I found that fascinating. I began collecting and comparing these stories to see how anxiety uses the tactics and how different people responded. These were the same ways anxiety worked on me in my life (Anxiety is a conniving little bugger!). I started sharing these findings with new people that I met, who found it helpful to see these tricks for what they are — lies. They reported that it helped them so much, because when they knew about them, the tactics weren't as convincing. Once they exposed the sneaky ways anxiety works, those ways no longer worked.

What are the tricks and tactics of fear? They are all of the ways anxiety exerts its power over you and tricks you into being afraid. Anxiety's whole goal in life is to get you to be scared and stuck. It's ruthless in its efforts to make you suffer so it can stay in your life. For example, one of the tricks of anxiety that I've already mentioned is having you feel like you are "out of control."

This is arguably the most disempowering belief that you can have, and disempowering you is exactly what the anxiety wants, because as long as you keep handing over your power, it rules. Here is one of my favorite quotes by Alice Walker.

> *"The most common way to give away your power*
> *is to think that you do not have any."*

Let's get your power back. We can start by looking at what disempowering tactics you're up against. Below are some examples of things anxiety might tell you.

You are weak because you have anxiety.

Something bad is going to happen.

You don't have the skills to feel better.

You are not going to be able to handle it.

You will freak out.

You will be so uncomfortable.

You can't do it.

You will always feel this way.

Anything sound familiar?

These are the lies that anxiety loves to tell, and you've become so accustomed to them that they can be very convincing truths. Anxiety has many tricks and tactics for keeping you beaten-down, confused and vulnerable so that sometimes you don't even know which end is up.

Tricks and Tactics of Anxiety

In this chapter, I expose fifteen typical tricks and tactics that anxiety uses. This exposure gives you some distance to see them for what they are when anxiety pitches them your way. Compiled from thousands of conversations, I can say that anxiety does the following.

1. Says, "I Protect You"
2. Uses Black and White Thinking
3. Evasively Threatens: "It Will Be Awful"
4. Insists: "This Is Real" or "This Is Important"
5. Convinces You That You Will Go Crazy
6. Discourages You by Saying: "There's No Point"
7. Makes You Forget What You Know

8. Scares You
9. Terrorizes You When You Are Vulnerable
10. Tells You That You Are Untrustworthy
11. Cuts You Down
12. Tries to Confuse You
13. Disguises Itself
14. Doesn't Want You to Talk About It Tells You: "You Can't Handle It"

Let's break down anxiety's hold by understanding these tricks so they never have the power over you again.

Trick #1: Anxiety Says, "I Protect You"

Avoiding danger is no safer in the long run than outright exposure. The fearful are caught as often as the bold.
~Helen Keller

Janice

Janice had seen many hard times in her past. Though her life was currently going okay, she was frequently filled with dread that something bad would happen again.

I asked what this was like for her and how it affected her life. She told me it preoccupied her, taking up a lot of her time and energy. It made her feel vulnerable and want to stay close to home. She also kept her heart "close to home," which meant avoiding getting close to people. This resulted in severe loneliness.

I asked her if it was okay that this "dread" took her time and energy, made her feel vulnerable and alone. She said no. I asked how she'd rather it be.

Janice said, "I would love to not worry about it." She paused and her brow furrowed as if she had just remembered something. "But… then something could happen and blindside me. No, no, if something goes wrong, I'd rather be prepared." I asked her how she prepares for this, but she couldn't tell me. I asked how expecting something awful would help her when that something awful happened, and she didn't know.

"I just feel better," she said.

I reminded Janice that she came to see me because she doesn't feel good about feeling so bad all of the time. I added, "How does feeling anxious and vulnerable, and as you described — terrified — day in and day out help you feel confident and competent when you're faced with a difficult event in the future?"

She just smiled.

"So you suffer day in and day out in the guise of protecting yourself in some unknown way from some future chance of suffering?"

People suffer through the frustration of not telling people how they feel, not trying for something they desire and not feeling better, because these things make them feel vulnerable. They avoid them in the hopes that they can keep their heart safe from being hurt. As I see it, they're *currently* suffering to avoid *possible* future suffering. People put up with this for years, convinced beyond a shadow of a doubt they're protecting themselves.

Wouldn't expecting the worst and living in anxiety make you *less* equipped to handle the bumps in life, not more? Your single best bet in handling the good, bad and worse situations is the opposite of anxiety — it's belief in yourself. When you trust that you can handle what comes your way, anxiety can't get you anymore.

Sam

Sam wanted to live free from the panic and anxiety that he'd struggled with for many years. He desired this more than anything, to the point he decided that if he couldn't find peace by his sixtieth birthday, it would be too late to ever feel better and he would give up and end his life. Except, he was also *afraid* of feeling better. He felt vulnerable and hated his emotions now, but at least this was suffering that he knew. Sam wasn't so sure what healing would feel like and worried that either the process of "feeling better" or the result "feeling better" might be unbearable. As he described it, he was "safe in his vulnerability." Sam found "suffering-so-intensely-that-he'd-rather-die-than-keep-suffering" familiar, and worried about healing, because it was unfamiliar. He dreaded that healing might be worse somehow, even though by definition *healed* is better.

This first trick is a doozy! When anxiety acts as if it has your best interest at heart and beguiles you with its confounding logic, it's hard to see through it. It's easy to believe anxiety protects you, because we know that biologically, fear's function is to protect us. While the emotion of fear is an invitation (it invites us to action by evoking awareness, passion and creativity), anxiety is a prison. That's why I'm so adamant about separating the two meanings. Fear has merits. Anxiety is when we get stuck in the sympathetic nervous system's response, even though there's no physical danger present. There is nothing good about it.

My own anxiety used this trick on me. I imagined that I was on a cliff and anxiety was a guard saying he was protecting me from falling. I had to stay put or else I might lose myself (or my sanity) forever over the side. Trusting anxiety's commands, I stayed frozen in panic, high on the cliff and isolated from my life, but apparently "safe."

Have you ever felt safe in your suffering? Anxiety can make it seem so rational and smart.

When I finally decided to get better, I knew that I had to let go of the pseudo "protection" of anxiety. Still, it felt counter-intuitive to jump off the cliff I'd been clinging onto for dear life. Falling felt totally out of control. Anxiety kept saying, "You don't know for sure it will be okay." But being trapped wasn't the way I wanted to live any longer.

I decided to jump off that imaginary cliff. I practiced many times in the beginning using guided imagery during meditation. Then, I began to take small risks in my real life, doing things I had been avoiding like eating in restaurants, traveling and going to the movies. It was a leap of faith. I trusted that whatever I found at the bottom had to be better than this and whatever it was, I could handle it.

It ended up being an escape from anxiety into freedom and joy. What I had assumed for so long would be a *loss* of control, gained me more control than I'd had in years. I was allowed to do more things that made me happy.

We believe surrendering will leave us more vulnerable or even make us insane, but it actually leads us to feeling less vulnerable — more confident and connected to our skills.

I spent a lot of years trying to outrun or outsmart vulnerability by making things certain and definite, black and white, good and bad. My inability to lean into the discomfort of vulnerability limited the fullness of those important experiences that are wrought with uncertainty: Love, belonging, trust, joy, and creativity to name a few.

~Brené Brown

Sam also began using the metaphor of a cliff when he talked about his feelings. He assumed at the bottom of his cliff was permanent insanity or certain death, just like me. He was torturing himself being anxious and miserable trying to protect himself from going over the side.

I told him about my imaginary anxiety cliff and how I focused on letting go in guided meditation. We began working on Sam's anxiety in the same way. Safely in our imaginations, we held hands and jumped off his cliff and sailed gently into a pool of warm water. We floated awhile, feeling healed and energized. We looked at the clouds and beautiful landscape around us, and Sam felt supported and relieved that this was the opposite of what he'd thought it would be. He felt better and more free than he had in years. This process built up his confidence and he, too, started to take that confidence into conscious actions in his life.

The fear response was biologically created to protect you. You may think that it's "worry" that has you being careful, but I'd rather just call this good sense.

Anxiety, though? Anxiety doesn't protect you at all.

Take action

Do this Cliff Guided Meditation: Read the following and allow yourself 10–20 minutes to meditate on it.

Get yourself in a relaxed position, lying down or sitting comfortably. Close your eyes and relax into your body, following your breath for a couple of minutes. Once you feel settled and calm, use your imagination to picture yourself on a high cliff of darkness and despair. You may feel afraid and alone here, but also scared to fall off the cliff, thinking it would be the end of you. Imagine your inner wisdom, me, or a best friend there with you. Our guidance comes from love and trust, and we trust you so much more than you do yourself right now. We tell you that it's okay to be vulnerable — that you can handle it. We assure you that you will feel less vulnerable if you leave this cliff and return to life. Take your time to fill yourself with faith and trust. Then, imagine holding our hands and leaping off the cliff together. There's no chaos in our fall. We feel a gentle breeze and softly land into warm, clear water only a few yards off a beautiful bright beach. The darkness and despair are gone and we splash and relax, invigorated by the water and enjoying the natural beauty that surrounds us. We laugh and smile at each other.

Trick #2: Anxiety Uses Black and White Thinking

Stephanie

"This morning I yelled at Robbie, because he peed on the kitchen floor and I'm wondering if that's healthy," Stephanie asked me over the phone when our kids were young. My son Leo was a little older, so I guess I was a veteran at potty training.

Stephanie wanted to know if she was *exactly* healthy or exactly *not* healthy. Black and white thinking is clean and simple. Everything is wrapped up neatly. The boundaries are perfectly clear so that we can never, ever make a mistake.

It's like this. You're either normal or abnormal, perfect or a failure, healthy or unhealthy. Then, you judge things that happen as either good or bad, healed or unhealed. And only if you can be *sure* of the positive, you can properly put things in their place since there's no doubt or anxiety that you've gotten it wrong. Only then can you relax knowing you're "okay."

Except you can't. Because perfect, normal and healthy are indefinable. Such absolute values don't exist in a world where everything is relative.

It's scientifically proven that everything we see, feel and know in this universe is relative depending on how it interacts with other things. Our thoughts are relative to our perception. Our physical body changes in response to stimuli in our external and internal environments. Molecules change. Matter changes. And, as Albert Einstein[15] proved in his *Theory of Relativity*, even space and time can change. There's only one exception to this — the speed of light. As far as scientists understand at the moment, light is different from every other thing in the universe in that it stays constant and absolute no matter what. None of these black and white standards that we measure ourselves against are as constant as *light*. When you

---

15   Albert Einstein and Robert Lawson, *Relativity: The Special and General Theory* (Seattle: Mockingbird Classics Publishing. 2015).

set a standard for yourself that is absolute (such as perfection) you'll never be satisfied, because achieving it is impossible. This will leave you feeling not good enough, it'll have you not trusting yourself and vulnerable to anxiety.

Stephanie is trying to define her whole self by this one moment. I answer her, "If you tell me what 'healthy' is, I'll let you know. What I do know is that you're a wonderfully kind and loving mom. I yell, too. You've had so much patience through this process, you're doing great. Robbie is lucky to have you. I love you to pieces!" I sidestepped the impossible standard, did my best to debunk it for her and instead pointed out her skills and the values that she mothers by. This acknowledges her worth and connects her with how she wants to be.

If you believe black and white thinking keeps you safe, it doesn't. When there's no middle ground, you'll always be vulnerable to the threat of failure. The definition of success is so specific that you have such a small chance — if any — of achieving it. This has you perceiving yourself as failing even before your try. Many people want to hold on to this "threat of failing" because they see it as motivating, but it's only motivating when you see the flexibility of shades of gray. Black and white thinking has you frozen. You're exhausted like you ran a marathon, but you've gotten nowhere.

Leslie

Leslie was emotionally and physically abused growing up. Because her abusers used anger to fuel and justify their violence, Leslie perceives anger as absolutely dangerous and so now it always provokes anxiety.

This affects her current relationships. Her friends, her bosses and her kids are human and sometimes feel angry. Even if they express this appropriately, there's no ground for Leslie to feel safe. When there is anger, she feels vulnerable and wholly responsible because she failed at keeping the person happy, even if the anger has nothing to do with her. Leslie concludes that she's unlovable and has lost that relationship forever. This is emotionally devastating and her panic increases.

What's worse is that anxiety is present even before anyone is angry, because Leslie is constantly vigilant and working hard to prevent it, worried that it might happen anyway. She can't really trust herself, because Leslie believes she's failed at keeping people happy in the past — not only her abusers, but everyday people having bad days. But this same imperfection means that she could be attacked, so she exhausts herself attempting to be perfectly *good enough* even though she doesn't expect to make it.

Desperate, she is trying to overcome panic by outrunning failure that she is certain she'll have anyway, when nothing has even happened yet. She's on a hamster wheel, a no-win situation. Perfection doesn't exist. Within the parameters she's created, she could never feel safe, even when she is.

This is physically and emotionally exhausting. On top of that, Leslie is humiliated by her behavior, which makes her feel totally messed up. When nothing you do is good enough, you come to the conclusion that you're not likable, lovable or trustworthy, and that conclusion seems inescapably true. When it is "true," there is *no* escape. You feel different and wrong and it affects your self-esteem, creating a vicious cycle further lowering your confidence and faith in yourself. This is an invitation for anxiety to reign over your life. Despair is just waiting to overtake you. You feel worthless.

If you understand that there are shades of gray, this can all change. You'll accept yourself with all of your imperfections, knowing they are temporary and relative, that everyone has them and they don't define all of you. Leslie's skills in preventing, detecting and protecting herself from anger were lifesaving when she was in her abusive situation. In our work together we honored them for their service, instead of judging them as crazy. But now, she is relearning about anger, seeing its relativity in different contexts. She's relieved to understand that she could make someone mad, but it's temporary. The person could still love her and forgive her and this exchange could improve her relationships by releasing pent-up feelings, allowing deeper understanding and helping both parties support each other better.

When you're not limited by black and white thinking, you'll understand that you are more than your imperfections. Take Stephanie. She can connect with herself as a loving, patient and kind mother, who cares so much for Robbie, rather than believe that she is just *unhealthy*.

If you see things as relative, you no longer view yourself as a complete failure. You give yourself the opportunity to embrace your skills and learn more about your values. This will grow trust in yourself. You will feel better and less vulnerable in life.

Take action

Practice seeing different perspectives. This will help you understand there are many ways to look at a situation; some could be negative to you, and others are not. There are no truths in perception, just ideas.

First, think about an event you've experienced recently. Then, write down seven possible explanations for that. Get creative!

Example 1: Tammy was rude to me last week.
1. She is preoccupied with a problem at work.
2. I caught her off guard.
3. She was in a hurry and didn't mean to be short with me.
4. She might have misunderstood something I said.
5. She was tired or hungry.

6. She doesn't like me.

7. I upset her.

Example 2: I didn't get the job I was interviewed for.

1. The other candidate knew someone.

2. It wasn't a good fit.

3. My resume had a typo.

4. I was only partly what they were looking for.

5. There was high competition.

6. I didn't have the right qualifications.

7. There is something else coming along.

Event_____

_____

_____

_____

_____

_____

_____

Trick #3: Anxiety Evasively Threatens "It Will Be Awful!"

Check out this conversation I often had with Anxiety.

Anxiety: You have to do this or else.

Me: Or else what?
Anxiety: Or else something bad will happen.
Me: What will happen?
Anxiety: Something really bad.
Me: What?
Anxiety: You will hate it.
Me: What is it?
Anxiety: It will be awful.
Me: What will?

I didn't know what would be so awful and anxiety didn't tell me, but it sounded bad. When anxiety had me trapped in its grasp, I wouldn't even challenge it like this. Back then, anxiety had me at, "You have to do this or else." I was on my cliff saying, "Yes, sir, thank you, sir!"

During the years of interviewing people with anxiety, I had a different perspective. With clients I was outside the chaos and fear of anxiety and I could ask these questions. I started to realize that anxiety is one evasive dude! There was never a straight answer, just a lot of skirting around. And I started to see the power anxiety had over people by doing this. The evasiveness is part of the public relations plan anxiety has to hold the monopoly on your life. Evasiveness is anxiety's trademark. The mystique gives it power.

But this is a very thin veil that anxiety hides behind. It's like the wizard in the *Wizard of Oz*, saying, "Pay no attention to that man behind the curtain." It doesn't want you to uncover its fraudulent claims, because this would take away its power. But anxiety's lies about the awful things happening are just like the illusion of the floating wizard head — no substance. It's just a weak threat of something evasively awful.

So I started to challenge anxiety's frequent demands — that I had to stay home, make my house look perfect, eat perfectly healthy and avoid risks like travel or any sort of fun. I became like a child responding to his mother's requests asking, "But why?"

Anxiety uses evasiveness to get you to anticipate something scary. But through my many, many interviews, I've discovered that anticipatory anxiety is usually worse than the discomfort that it taunts you with. First of all, it exists now, when the object of fear hasn't and may never happen. Second, you're helpless in anticipatory anxiety, because nothing is happening, so there is nothing to do to help yourself. Anticipatory anxiety can last months and years. It's very intense.

Bad things do happen to us, but usually much less often and causing less difficulty than our anxiety has us expecting. Besides, human history has proven over and over that people do get through the hard times they experience. They keep busy creating ways to survive, distracting themselves and resisting any oppression. This keeps their minds occupied and feeling purposeful, rather than immobilized by helplessness. People feel less anxious during the difficult event than when they anticipated it happening.

When people are in abusive relationships and sense that their abuser is getting tense, they sometimes instigate the abuse to get it over with. They know they can handle the abuse, since they have before, but the anticipation of it coming is overwhelming to their psyche. To anticipate *the worst* every day causes much more suffering.

Bella was in high school and afraid of falling on the ice and embarrassing herself. We unpacked the likelihood of this statistically, but she said, "What if I'm the one it happens to?" I've seen that "What if?" really do a number on people. It's an excuse to be afraid. Anxiety uses that remote chance to freak you out, saying, *What if that is you? What if you fall and it is awful?*

Next time anxiety does this to you, ask yourself, *What is the worst that can happen?* Then, keep asking yourself, *What is bad about that happening? And what is bad about that? Why is that so bad?*

Don't take its evasive garbage! You want answers. When you see that anxiety can't give you answers, you'll know that you have nothing to be afraid of. Keep asking and you'll realize it's less of a big deal than you thought.

Anxiety is especially evasive with OCD. It tells people that someone might die if their bed is not made properly, but doesn't explain what the possible connection is between the two. No one bothers finding out how hospital corners could save a life, because if there is a remote chance it's true, you'll do all that you can. We are more scared of that general threat than we would be of small realistic things that actually could happen.

Jack

Jack worked in the maintenance department at a golf course. He used a cart to get around the property. When he left the vehicle for any reason, he worried that he left it running, having to come back and check multiple times that the engine was off.

To break down this anxiety, I asked him what was the worst that would happen if it was idling. He didn't have an answer to this so I ran down the possible consequences, asking him if he was afraid of each: *It might run out of gas? Someone might catch you being negligent? The cart will drive away without you? You will get fired?*

He admitted that he wouldn't want these to happen, but his anxiety didn't torment him with these. He simply didn't worry that they would happen. But anxiety told him, "It'll be *bad* if you left the cart running. You have to check it or I won't leave you alone," and that clinched it. Seeing that there was nothing behind it helped Jack break through anxiety's hold. This helped him reason himself out of the compulsion.

We are so darn scared of being disappointed. Anxiety has us freaking out trying to prevent it, but in reality, we're constantly disappointed and handle it all the time.

In life anything can happen. There will be amazing things, devastating things and everything in the middle. However, it will hardly ever be the awful, hot mess anxiety puts into your imagination.

Take action

Reflect on a worry that you have. Unpack it by asking it the following questions: *What's bad about that? What is bad about that happening? And what is bad about that? Why is that so bad? What if that happened, how bad would that be? What is the worst that could happen? What would that be like?*

_____

_____

_____

_____

_____

_____

Trick #4: Anxiety Insists: "This Is Real" or "This Is Important"

Each time you get anxious, does your mind tell you that this time you *really* have something to be worried about? Here are some examples.

This semester is really going to be difficult, because I have some more difficult professors than before.

This time anxiety is being truthful, because I really could lose her.

I caused this, so I should be worried.

When you think your anxiety is valid and should be there, it would be pretty illogical of you to let it go. Keeping it seems like the intelligent option. But, keeping it is suffering.

Did you ever hear people distinguish between rational fear and irrational fear? Making a fear "rational" just gives the anxiety more power.

Samantha

Before Samantha (the young girl who was afraid of losing her mom) came to me, many members of her family were curious about how she was so strong through all the troubling times only to be immobilized in panic once everything was peaceful. Her school counselor offered Samantha the explanation, "You were too young before and didn't understand the serious nature of the events when they were happening. Now you understand and that's why you're afraid."

This elevated Samantha's anxiety. Being validated by an adult, essentially gave her the message, *Now you are smart enough to know you are supposed to be afraid. You should be afraid of these things.* Anxiety is constructed as "real," associating it with being more mature, more knowledgeable and more rational.

Samantha's anxiety is understandable given all she went through. It was useful for her to reflect on how these events recruited anxiety into her life. When we did this, it helped her comprehend and have compassion for herself ("I understand why I wouldn't want to lose my mom."), but it didn't validate it. Validating it is saying, *You should feel anxious.*

Samantha isn't anxious because she is too weak or incapable of handling what happens. Anxiety just gets out of hand and feeds on itself. It can happen to anyone, anytime. It commonly happens to people after they've made it through a difficult situation, because they had something to *survive* during the crisis. That action used up the fear response energy and they felt empowered and purposeful even through the awfulness of it all. After the hard time, the body hasn't fully recovered and still releases stress hormones triggered by thoughts of the past or something happening again — but there's nothing to do now, because nothing is really happening. A sense of helplessness arises and anxiety can begin to take hold.

On the other hand, if you find something to do during the recovery period, you can prevent anxiety from gaining momentum. Then, you can disempower your anxiety by breaking down why it is there and what it means.

One way we know anxiety is not real is that it is inconsistent. Anxiety told Samantha that she ought to be scared about cancer when her mother was absent but not when she was present. Anxiety makes this idea seem rational, but it is not logical. You can't stop cancer by proximity. When we are feeling anxious, it's hard to see the inconsistencies in anxiety's arguments. But it is constantly switching tactics to find your vulnerabilities. If it's saying one thing here and another thing there, how can you trust that *anything* it's saying is true?

Keith

I was supervising a social worker who works in a hospital for critically ill children. She asked me how to help Keith, a little boy whose brother just died. She was curious about how to rid him of his "real" fear of dying too. Her reasoning was that he has the same blood disorder as his late brother, so his fear was "rational." This seems to make sense at first but with that argument each and every one of her patients, being critically ill, ought to have anxiety. But even though she'd been working there for ten years, she was totally stumped by this little guy.

We're all going to die and rarely do we know how or when. Also, something bad could and probably will happen to you in your lifetime. You could lose someone, get hurt, get robbed or be embarrassed. These things are possible, and it is understandable and biological to fear them. But if we lived in perpetual anxiety over them, life would stink.

The difference between people who live in continual fear and people who don't is that the anxious people give the fear their attention. They *think* about being afraid. This was me. One time, for seven months prior to a trip, each night I sat in my bedroom and panicked that my plane would crash.[16] I gave it so much attention and energy, because it made sense to be afraid. I couldn't resolve it because any way I sliced it, crashing would be awful. But I was miserable living with this panic that consumed my days.

Dread becomes so great that we lose any faith in ourselves to get through any hard situation. Remember in Trick #2, Anxiety Uses Black and White Thinking, we learned that anticipating a bad thing is many times worse than the bad thing itself. Everyone is afraid of something bad happening too, but rather than dwell on it, they focus on other things.

Assessing fear as rational or irrational is one more way to get you *off* the path to feeling better. It's distracting and holds your attention on anxiety. Thinking a fear is rational has you fighting to keep anxiety.

Argue for your limitations and,
sure enough, they're yours.
~Richard Bach

---

16   How I got over my fear of flying: jodiaman.com/conquer-your-fear-of-flying/.

Fear is relative. Fear is not rational or irrational. It is not real or imagined, logical or illogical, valid or invalid. Fear is merely an experience. It may be an intense experience and have many unappreciated effects on your life, but it's still just an experience. Argue that your anxiety is *right* and you get to keep it. Think of it differently and you can let it go.

Take action

What are some ways your anxiety has made you believe that it's real and you *should* feel scared?

_____

_____

_____

_____

_____

_____

Trick #5: Anxiety Convinces You That You Will Go Crazy

Sam

Sam (from Trick #1) used to email me between sessions in a state of panic. He understood and named his feelings as "emotionally crashing." He felt like he was losing touch with reality and things were totally out of his control. These are emails he wrote.

Jodi,

I want to wish you a Merry Christmas. I understand if you don't get this until after tomorrow but I need you to know that I'm crashing fast!

Jodi,

Today it hit me hard and I feel extremely overwhelmed. I know I always think that this one is the worst ever and it feels that way again. For the first time in a long time suicide has come back up. I HATE these feelings. They take me over. I've been crying on and off all day. Shaking all over.

Hi Jodi,

Thank you for yesterday's session. It's giving me a lot to think about. However I'm finding myself slipping today. Everything feels unreal. Like I am watching everything happening, but I am not a part of it. I've taken my medicine and listened to your message, but I'm finding it hard to do anything to help myself. Why can't I figure this out?

When you experience emotions, your mind seeks to figure them out. If those feelings are overwhelming, you might decide you're losing it, breaking down, plummeting, shutting down, spiraling out of control or losing touch with reality. These are scary descriptions and can make you feel like

you are having a nervous breakdown, which triggers more anxiety. You're pulled over the edge of the insanity cliff and panic that you'll never have control over your life — you'll never be okay again. On top of that, you're ashamed of being considered mentally ill.

It took me a few of Sam's emails to figure out that he was having panic attacks, since he didn't use those words. Once we renamed what he was experiencing as anxiety, his fear over the episodes decreased significantly. A temporary panic attack is much easier to handle than an emotional collapse.

Dear Sam,

Think about the words "slipping" and "overwhelmed." They disempower you and make the anxiety worse. Try to use "It's an anxiety attack and I've gone through it before."

Hugs,

Jodi

I've talked many people down from panic attacks, most of them worrying they'd lost touch with reality just like Sam. They described feeling totally disconnected from the world around them, seeing objects in their presence as surreal. From my perspective, it was easy to see that they weren't crazy — they were speaking rationally and clearly, but they were terrified about what they felt.

I remembered from my own panicky days how I felt different and disconnected, too. It totally charged up my panic, making me feel even *more* disconnected and then more anxious and then *more* disconnected... Feeling disconnected is very scary. It gives you the message that you've lost it and you're different from other people. This meaning — *I'm crazy* — is even scarier than the feeling, which is scary enough.

The reason you feel like you've lost touch with reality is because the hormones released during anxiety put you into a state of hyperawareness. If you were watching a movie that wanted to give you the feeling of hyperawareness, it would shift the scene as if you were watching it through a tunnel, or a blur, or skew the audio so it sounds bizarre. If you stared at a cup on your table, really focusing on it, it would begin to look bizarre, too. When you say a word over and over, like "squirrel," the hyperawareness of the word eventually makes the sound of it strange to you.

Try it right now. Say "squirrel" ten times. It's a very weird word when you look at it closely, isn't it? If you're in a state of hyperawareness, everything you think and see starts to seem bizarre or unreal. This is not a pathological condition. People meditate on purpose to get themselves to this state. But if anxiety brings you there without your consent, it can be unsteadying until you can see it for what it is and that you're not losing your mind.

Things changed for Sam after our discovery. Before, he'd been crashing a few times a week with a greater intensity each time, but after, knowing anxiety was the cause took away the fear and judgment. Anxiety depends on these to keep its power. Sam began to recover faster and the length between the episodes grew longer. Rather than spending his energy in a downward spiral thinking he failed at life, he put energy into practices to decrease his body's stress response. He took walks during lunch and in the evenings. He joined a yoga class and he began to meditate.

If you feel like you're losing your mind, I understand. I've been there and I can assure you, you are *not* losing your mind. Try to remind yourself that it's simply hormones putting you in a state of hyperawareness. Try to laugh at the bizarreness of something like the word "squirrel" to lighten your mood. Usually when we go through life, we're too distracted by our daily chores and happenings to be hyperaware. Get back involved in what you need to be doing that day. Take a walk outside if you can, to use up some of the nervous energy. Before you know it, you'll be feeling better.

Take action

Take a walk outside today. If it's cold out, bundle up. The exercise will warm you from within. Check your level of anxiety 1–10 before you leave and then again after you are finished. Did your anxiety go down at all?

Watch my video on 5 Ways Nature Helps with Anxiety on YouTube or find it easily on the book resource page, jodiaman. com/you1anxiety0.

Trick #6: Anxiety Discourages You by Saying: "There's No Point"

The purpose of life is to live it, to taste experience to the utmost, to reach out eagerly and without fear for newer and richer experience."

~Eleanor Roosevelt

When I was anxious, it would often be triggered sitting in a restaurant. I had no reason for feeling in danger while eating out, but anxiety doesn't need much of a reason. The first time it happened, I was out with my family eating wonderful food. All of a sudden I became hyperaware that I was full. I worried that I would be uncomfortably full and that I'd get nauseous. I worried that it would trigger anxiety and I would "lose it tonight." As you might expect, worrying about anxiety fed it and boom — it came on strong!

And so, anxiety latched itself on to restaurant dining. All it took was a small pang in my stomach for me to worry, and anxiety would take over for the evening. I responded like anyone might — I avoided restaurants.

When I would get invited out, I'd imagine what problems might arise and it seemed so awful and uncomfortable that it wasn't worth the trouble. Having fun, eating good food and connecting to close friends paled in comparison to the priority of avoiding anxiety. There seemed to be no *good* point to going out to a restaurant that made any difference. It was just easier to stay home.

Jessica

Jessica felt the same. She landed a new job in a printing shop. She was grateful for the opportunity, really excited about the creative atmosphere and loved her new boss. Two weeks in, doubt took up residence in her mind. It was reminding her how she screwed up many times in the past, because anxiety and depression made her miss work and lose good jobs. She began to have trouble getting out of bed and had been late a couple of times already. Soon she was having trouble getting herself going at all.

Doubt had her so convinced that she would mess this job up, there didn't seem to be any point in *trying* to keep it, so she went back to sleep.

Anxiety has a way of shooting down the point of doing things. It tells you that things aren't worth the effort. I enjoyed restaurants before anxiety attached to them. But after, it wasn't worth the suffering. I'm not alone. People don't want to do something that causes suffering.

A few years ago, my hometown of Rochester was the location for filming a few scenes in the *Spider-Man 2* movie. The whole city was abuzz. Everyone was going downtown to watch the filming and I decided to take my kids. Leo was immediately excited, but quickly decided that he didn't want to go. When I asked why, he said, "I don't know."

What preteen boy who is hugely into superheroes and comics wouldn't want to go to watch one filmed live? *An anxious one.* He didn't know what it would be like, and it wasn't worth risking being stuck somewhere that he might be uncomfortable.

Why would you want to do something that's unpleasant and not enjoyable? You wouldn't. Even if you start out wanting to do something, like Jessica, it's easy to get discouraged and decide there's no point in trying, because you won't succeed anyway. You go so far as to tell yourself that you don't want to do anything. It's easier to not want to do it, than to feel sad because you missed it. When others invite you out, you insist, "I don't feel like it." And, you don't have an answer when your loved ones ask, "Why not?"

That evasiveness (Trick #3) is a telltale sign that anxiety might be present. It's easier to think that *you don't want to* than to accept that anxiety is not letting you. But is this the truth? If you could be assured that you wouldn't get anxiety there, would you go?

When anxiety is present, I understand that comfort becomes your top priority. I get that becoming calm again is the most important thing ever. Your anxiety says, "You can do that once you're comfortable," to pacify you into staying still. But if you listen to anxiety, you'll never be comfortable and never be able to move.

Finding courage over anxiety is easy, if you uncover something that's important enough to supersede anxiety's demands. I knew a girl who could barely leave her house due to social anxiety. She didn't go to school for years and the adults in her life decided that she wasn't emotionally capable of attending. Until she joined the girl's hockey team. She loved it! The biggest bonus was the district rule — if she missed school, she couldn't go to hockey practice. After years of school avoidance, she went to school every day during the season. Hockey was that important.

Even with anxiety, I would go to a restaurant when it was important, like a birthday or family celebration. You might be afraid of hospitals, but if you need to get your child medical care you'd go in one. Helping your baby is the priority. What we value gives us courage over our fears. The stronger the "point" of an activity, the easier it will be to overcome your anxiety and do it.

There can be one — or more than one — point to anything. Having fun, achieving a goal, gaining something, being responsible or problem solving. Sometimes the point is more sublime, like helping others, raising self-confidence or building relationships. Often it's joy that's the most essential point of doing anything in life. Joy is very important to me and was a big motivator when I was overcoming anxiety. Life doesn't seem worth putting up with, if joy doesn't break up the hard times.

Anxiety zaps the joy out of life. That wasn't okay with me. I don't think it's okay with *you*. You deserve joy. Make it a priority. Ask yourself, is living free important enough to knock satisfying-anxiety's-demands down a notch? You bet it is!

Take action

List what is more important to you than satisfying the anxiety.

Trick #7: Anxiety Makes You Forget What You Know

Leslie

When Leslie (from Trick #2) feels ashamed of herself, she withdraws from the world and even me. We've known each other for years and she's shared with me her deepest, darkest secrets. In all that time, she's worried that sharing each event in her life history would cause me to be disappointed in her, because they made her disappointed in herself. She also worried that she was betraying me if she was sad one day.

Shame is overwhelming to the human psyche. It holds us down and gives us a sense of not belonging, since we're not good enough to belong. This negative self-judgment, making us feel like we've failed at being "acceptable," is heavy on our hearts and bodies. On top of making us vulnerable to anxiety, it has us suffering immense grief over ruining our own life. When shame is around, we crave connection, but since we feel undeserving of it, this longing creates more shame. Even feeling sad or anxious opens a floodgate of self-deprecation, because this is not allowed either. But then again, since we've screwed up so much, we're also banned from being happy. With shame, you have nowhere to stand. You can't be sad, you can't be happy, you can't connect and you can't separate. You blame yourself and you defend yourself, and neither is right. Intense shame is an emotional nightmare.

This is exactly how shame affects Leslie's life. In all of our time together, she has never disappointed me with her secrets and she's never let me down *because* she was feeling sad. With each doubt flare-up I reassure her that I have no negative feelings toward her, only greater compassion and understanding. She's relieved and grateful that I don't judge her. We play this record again and again.

Leslie is very intelligent. She is capable of remembering and creating an understanding of me from our history. But when doubt, shame and anxiety are around, this knowledge is forgotten. She worries that I will "leave her" this time. And since this would be devastating and there's nothing that she can do to prevent it, she begins to prepare and *protect* herself by pulling back (Trick #1).

"Anxiety makes you forget what you know" is a very common tactic uncovered while interviewing many people about their anxieties. While we unpacked their worries, I questioned the likelihood of their worst fear coming true. Over and over, their answers displayed common sense, sharp intelligence and all kinds of solid evidence about why their worries were ridiculous, unwarranted and unnecessary.

There are statistically very few plane crashes.
The doors are locked.
I have done it before.
It's unlikely it will happen.
It wasn't so bad last time.
I keep myself healthy.
Bridges rarely collapse for no reason.

What happens to this intelligence, I wondered, when anxiety is around? Anxiety blocks us from what we know as a tactic to stay in power. Your intelligence would reassure, calm and soothe you when anxiety is trying to upset you about some remote near-impossibility.

Even though she's seen me be compassionate with other people's sadness, Leslie's anxiety convinced her I would get aggravated with *hers*. It also made her forget a lot of other things she knew would make her feel better.

When you fear that someone will leave you, you forget that he or she loves you. When you're afraid of getting through a day of school, you forget that you've done it before. When you are afraid of failing, you forget that you usually get another chance. Life can be pretty terrifying when you forget these things.

Leslie was so accustomed to doubt and anxiety that her brain was easily triggered by them. Now she's working on retraining her brain. I helped her create a list of her skills and knowledges.

Leslie's Skills and Knowledges

I know...

...Jodi cares about me.

...I am good at my job.

...I am smart.

...I have made good decisions.

...I eat healthy.

...I have something to contribute to the world.

...I care about people's feelings.

...People appreciate that I care about them.

...and so on.

I suggested that Leslie read this list three times a day when she's feeling content and calm. This is what I did helping myself. After a few days, she could also look at it when she's anxious to help calm her.[17] Because she is reading it so often, these skills and knowledges will stick in her brain and be right at the surface. When anxiety tries to outwit her, they will be harder to forget. If they're there to counter the lies of anxiety, it will begin to affect the stress hormone response of the brain and the physical nervousness will decrease each time, helping Leslie feel better.

It also raises her self-confidence, reminding Leslie of the skills she successfully employs in life. These skills become even more accessible with this confidence and life gets much easier from there.

17　Many people have testified that if they look at their lists when they are calm, this makes a significant difference in decreasing their anxiety overall. They report that if they only look at them when they are upset, the lists have little to no effect, short term or long term.

Take action

Write down what you know about yourself, your abilities, your family or your career. Read it over and over. Do this when you're calm. Then when the anxiety comes, it's at the forefront of your mind and harder to forget.

_____

_____

_____

_____

_____

_____

_____

Trick #8: Anxiety Scares You

You'll have noticed in many of these tricks that I acknowledge anxiety is scary. This is a tactic, too. Anxiety needs you to be scared in order for it to stay in power. Check out these two different responses to having a panic attack.

Person A: Oh, no. Something is wrong with me! It's happening again. I hate this. I wish this didn't happen. Why does this always happen to me? I hate this feeling! I'm going to have a heart attack. This is going to push me further down! My week is ruined, because this will take me so long to recover. I'm going to be like this forever. I can't take it. How am I going to live like this?

Person B: Hmmm, this is interesting, I am having an anxiety attack. Wow, it's intense... It feels pretty weird, though. I'm glad it will go away soon. I just have to get my body to calm down. It's been a stressful day. There is loads of stuff going on. I'm overtired and had too much caffeine. I had better take care of myself and get some sleep tonight.

Person A and Person B think about their anxious experience in very different ways. These different interpretations of the same physical feeling make or break their day. Anxiety's ability to snow-ball or fizzle out depends on how you think about it.

People jump out of planes to get an adrenaline rush. They call it a "thrill," and they love it. An anxious person might call a similar adrenaline rush "terror." They have the same physiological feelings, but apply different meanings.

There are two common ways you can experience anxiety. The first way is what I call "temporary anxiety," which isn't to suggest that the alternate form of anxiety is *permanent*. All anxiety is transient, meaning it never stays the same from one moment to another. Here, I'm using the word "temporary" to describe how a person might sense the anxiety he or she is experiencing. Like Person B, some people expect it to be temporary. They know they will be all right again once the anxious moment passes.

In this temporary form, the panic steals your present, making you desperate to be other than where you are and wishing for the feeling to be gone. But, knowing that it *will* pass and you'll be all right again decreases the suffering and intensity of the attack. In this way, you're less afraid of it.

Anxiety that ruins your *life* is much more fear-provoking than anxiety that ruins an hour or a day. Confidence it's a temporary attack can get you through it faster.

The second way you can sense anxiety is with the belief and expectation that it's permanent or, at the very least, long-lasting. Like Sam worrying about being psychotic or falling off his insanity cliff. He was afraid he would never be okay again. This is terrifying and makes the anxiety so much more powerful.

With this second kind of anxiety, you begin to panic, then you picture yourself freaking out at all future events and the panic intensifies. It's scary to think you'll feel anxious again and again and again with little or no hope for relief. The fear intensifies like the snowball effect, making you more afraid, which makes you more afraid, which makes you *more* afraid...

At the start of an anxiety attack, the amygdala triggers hormones to release. If you've had anxiety in the past, the body remembers this feeling (the feeling of adrenaline and cortisol in your body) as a dangerous situation and triggers the amygdala again. Cognitively, you can see that there is no physical danger, but the moment feels so scary and out of control that it continues to perpetuate the process. The fight or flight hormones affect your thought process too, helping you focus. But when there is no danger, this can turn to a near-obsessively paying attention to the antics of anxiety, doubt and self-deprecation — all combining to make everything worse.

Even if you are physically safe, your mind interprets this emotional fear and stress as a threat and your sympathetic nervous system responds by continuing the stress hormone release.

If you're not afraid of the adrenaline and cortisol's effect on your body, like a skydiver or race car driver that thrives on the thrill they get from the rush, then your body would no longer be triggered and it would re-acclimate, putting the brakes on the stress hormones within minutes.

It's understandable why anxiety is fear-provoking. You're not crazy or weak for being afraid. Have compassion for yourself. It *feels* scary.

Here's where you have to do the heavy lifting. It's time to take action and engage your personal agency to override that fear by reminding yourself, despite the intensity you feel, that this is just a feeling and that you're safe. It's when you convince yourself that there is nothing to be afraid of that anxiety is stripped of its power. Then, the stress hormones shut off and you can feel your body and mind calm down.

Cara

Cara was afraid of having a babysitter look after her and her brother. She was near panicked about her parents leaving and she would do anything in her power — scream and beg — for her parents to change their plans and stay home. She was even nervous when her parents were home, because she was afraid of the anxiety she anticipated would come when they were gone. She expected herself to be trapped and overwhelmed with no one to help her.

In counseling, we listed out her skills and knowledges and she became quite excited about them.

Cara's Skills and Knowledges

Amanda [the babysitter] is fun and does projects with us.

When I am having fun the Worries aren't there.

Last time Amanda was here, I had fun.

My brother will be with me.

Mom and Dad will only be gone for two hours. That will go fast.

If I need to, I can call them.

Amanda likes me. I like her.

Mrs. Selner is home next door.

We can watch TV and have a snack.

If the Worries come, I don't have to listen to them.

Then, we thought how lucky it was that she was having a babysitter that night, because then she could practice. We pumped her up even more, saying things like, "I hope Anxiety comes tonight, because then you can practice getting rid of it! You can show it who's the boss. Ha! It won't stand a chance tonight!" We made feeling empowered fun.

If you want and hope and beg anxiety to *come*, it can't. It needs you to be afraid.

Take action

Write a goodbye letter to "Anxiety."[18] Here's an example.

Dear (or Not So Dear) Fear and Anxiety,

You are both the same to me, as is Guilt! You have run my life for way too long and I have had enough! I will no longer allow you to set my path in life. You have taken me down into the bowels of Hell and I refuse to live there any longer. You have made me feel worthless, incapable, stupid, and unlovable, and I will not tolerate it. You have taken my self-esteem and squashed it. You have made me believe that it is all my fault and I don't deserve anything better. But, I have discovered that you are a liar! Everything you put into my head is a lie.

Sometimes you whisper and sometimes you scream, but they are all lies about me and my place in this universe. I cannot and will not have a relationship with a liar, someone who sucks the very life out of me! I have been a coward in your presence. I have let you

18   More examples at jodiaman.com/you1anxiety0

do with me what you wish. You have hurt me thousands of times and I still allow you in my life. You have kept me down, telling me not to try anything new because I will fail. Telling me it's too late for me to grow, but grow I will! Telling me I am incapable of love! Incapable of handling challenging experiences! Telling me I cannot heal or heal others! Telling me that I am nothing without you! Well, no more! I am everything without you!

Since I've discovered exactly what you are, I no longer want you in my life! So go away! Forever!

If you insist on returning, each and every time I will send you packing! You cannot be a part of my life anymore. You have done nothing but hurt me over and over again. I will not accept that from anyone, least of all you! No matter what you say, no matter how deep inside me you get, I know that I am a worthy, capable and lovable person. And I know that as long as I keep sending you away, the less power you will have over me, until you wither away to the nothingness that you really are!

I refuse to believe your accusations or tolerate your disrespect! It's done! No matter what you do, it's done. You are no longer welcome in my life!

With all the strength of Truth and Love on my side,

James

Your turn.

Dear Anxiety,

_____

_____

_____

_____

_____

_____

_____

_____

Trick #9: Anxiety Terrorizes You When You Are Vulnerable

Your outer context (the stressful events in your life) creates anxiety. This means you can be more susceptible to experiencing anxiety when you're sick or tired, not taking care of yourself, have a history of trauma, are isolated or are feeling stressed.

Your inner contexts (your emotions and thoughts) create and sustain anxiety also. Negative thoughts and worries about yourself and the world encourage and offer validation for anxiety (*What if I mess up?*).

Anxiety takes advantage of you when you're stressed and uses your vulnerability against you. When you are down and out, you crave the protection that anxiety is pretending to offer you.

Experiencing emotional and/or physical trauma has devastating effects on our bodies and minds.

Mary

Mary experienced sexual abuse by a teenage uncle when she was seven years old. She remembers the abuse and recalls feeling utterly powerless and terrified. The intensity of this experience imprints the memory in her mind and creates several problems.

The first is that the abuse is chaotic and therefore nonsensical. Mary continues to question why it happened and wrestle with her primary conclusion that she may have "allowed it." This creates a negative self-image and has her not trusting herself.

The terror and the chaos are all that she remembers. This creates a body memory of danger which can be triggered by sights, sounds, smells and feelings similar to what she experienced during the trauma. When triggered, anxiety has Mary reliving the horrible events of the past so intensely it's as if it's happening right now. This is referred to as a flashback, and it's terrifying. Each of these issues feed anxiety, but in combination they explode anxiety. From there, the anxiety grows and grows.

The memory of terror and chaos is only part of her story. It's about what happened to her. Narrative Therapy founder Michael White refers to this as a half-memory, because there is a significant part missing. The other half of the memory is Mary's response to the situation — the things she did in the moment, then right after or later — to survive the situation. Humans are biologically and emotionally programmed to survive. In any given situation when we are oppressed (overpowered), we protest that in some way. It could happen in our thoughts (defensiveness, anger, blame, conviction) or be expressed through action. These actions could be positive or negative, designed to protect ourselves, rebel, protect

---

19   Hugo Gorringe and Irene Rafael, "The Embodiment of Caste Oppression, Protest and Change," *Sociology* 41, no. 4 (February 2007): 97–114.

someone else, change, seek success or even give up. Throughout history, in any context of oppression,[19] there has been some human protest somewhere.

This is how I knew Mary had another half of her story. She must have protested her abuse in some way, so I asked her. Mary told me that once the abuse started, she tried to avoid playing with her uncle and cousins when she went to her grandmother's house, instead staying in the kitchen having tea with the women. She also refused to use the guest bathroom, because she knew about a peephole her uncle used to watch her through — one time having nowhere else to pee, but her grandmother's bedroom floor.

These were outstanding acts of protests at seven-years-old; however, they were rendered insignificant since she was shamed by the adults and ridiculed by her uncle for these behaviors. Unrecognized and unseen, as a way to protect herself, she even thought of her behaviors as pathological (peeing on the floor). To me, these responses were amazing, and they spoke volumes on what was important to Mary and the skills and courage she displayed in the attempt to protect herself at that young age. I asked Mary what these actions said about what she valued. Mary realized that she was important to herself. She knew her worth and that she was deserving of being safe.

She had a rich description of what happened to her, and now she had a rich description of her response. She could integrate both halves of the story together to make the memory of her abuse a whole memory. "Being empowered with skills" replaced "being a victim and vulnerability." This settled the chaos and helped quell some of that blame and questioning that kept Mary spiraling in her suffering. When you're empowered, anxiety loses its power.

A history of trauma is not a life sentence of anxiety. You can change the memory of a situation to a whole memory, significantly altering how you feel about that past experience. Even the traumatic body-memories that trigger the amygdala can be shifted and reprogrammed. Anxiety loves for us to be vulnerable. But vulnerability is relative. It's a state of awareness that is changeable. You feel vulnerable, because you *think* that you are vulnerable, just like you feel scared because you think something is scary. If you didn't think that you were vulnerable or saw vulnerability differently, you would become more comfortable. One way to feel less vulnerable is to remember your personal agency. You are not a passive recipient in this world. You are always responding. You have one hundred percent control over that response, and that response affects your life more than anything that can possibly happen to you.

Even something not traumatic, like having a to-do list a mile long with very little time to get it done, makes you feel unsettled and vulnerable. Anxiety loves these times in your life. If you feel overwhelmed about finishing a project, you obsess and worry that it won't go well. You suffer so much thinking about how hard it will be. You delay doing the project or never even begin, convinced there's no point to putting the effort in since you'll fail anyway.

After all of this worry and grief, if you *do* attempt the project, you're beyond exhausted and can have little or no energy for the actual tasks at hand. This is how anxiety keeps you feeling powerless.

Dealing with anxiety is a power game. Either you have the power or anxiety does. And that can change constantly depending on how you think. You can *think* yourself more powerful.

Connecting with your personal agency helps you rethink vulnerability and has you moving into a more empowered life.

Take action

Learn more about your vulnerability and your power. Start my free video series: **themaptowholepeace.com**

Trick #10: Anxiety Tells You That You Are Untrustworthy

I made decisions that I regret, and I took them as learning experiences... I'm human, not perfect, like anybody else.

~Queen Latifah

Anxiety tries to paralyze you from making any decisions by convincing you that you can't trust yourself. That's because anxiety can't persist in an environment where you take action and are decisive — you get things done and feel empowered. However confusing, anxiety has a survival instinct, just like you do.

If you can't make decisions, you can't take initiative or action. This leaves you feeling stuck and powerless. If you have a low opinion of yourself, you conclude that you can't handle situations and anxiety is able to rule your life. It often throws your past mistakes in your face to support its claims that you are untrustworthy, like Jane.

Jane

Jane thought she couldn't make any decisions. This belief became truth in her mind, because of three "mistakes" in her past. One was that she married the wrong guy — whom she divorced fifteen years ago. The second was having a cosmetic surgery twenty years earlier. The third was purchasing a boat that put her into deep debt — now long paid off. When she came to me, she was paralyzed when faced with even small decisions, because she identified herself as a "bad decision maker."

Humans make many small and large decisions every single day. Mistakes are hard to avoid; they happen to everybody. Luckily, they are usually only mildly annoying and don't matter too much (you forgot your lunch, you're wearing odd socks...).

It is how we think about mistakes that makes all the difference. Anxiety plagued Jane's life because she associated these decisions with shame. Anxiety capitalized on this shame and immobilized her from making any more decisions. She didn't trust that she could choose anything wisely, so she panicked when faced with every little choice.

Anxiety makes you feel trapped when faced with a decision, because you think you'll be trapped once you've *made* the choice and can never go back. In this scenario, you can't win. Make the choice, don't make the choice — either way, you lose. Anxiety tries to close off every avenue for movement, because keeping you stationary is how it keeps a hold on you. The desperation and panic that ensues is exhausting.

Nobody makes perfect decisions all the time. You make good ones sometimes and bad ones, too. Often, we're even confronted with decisions where there's more than one good option. The problem comes when you see these decisions, even small ones, in black and white. If you think that there's one right choice and one wrong one, you're stuck because you don't know which choice fits into the "absolutely right" category. Maybe you even start to think that smart people would know, and you are just too dumb. *How can you trust yourself, if you're dumb?*

You are not dumb. There is no "absolutely right" category. You just make a decision and adjust, if need be. For example, you have the budget for one pair of shoes, but find two pairs you like and have to choose to only buy one pair or go into debt. This kind of decision doesn't make or break your life. But anxiety can make you think that you could live to regret your decision. Even if you choose this time to charge the second pair and regret it, there are still ways to make that up and commit to making a different decision next time — you can return the shoes. You can prioritize paying it off, before any more optional spending. You can eliminate something else from your budget.

There are always more chances to rewrite our past decisions. A decision is not *over* because your life is not over. The chance may not be identical, but in the big picture view of your life, missed and taken chances usually come out in the wash. You see more of one or the other depending on the story you tell about your life. If you think that you're unlucky, you will see the missed opportunities. If you feel grateful for every little thing in your life, you will see your abundance.

I tried to unpack Jane's anxious beliefs. "Jane, in your forty-five years, have you made any other decision?"

"I don't know." Jane couldn't even trust herself to answer this question. So I helped her.

"In the last forty-five years have you received an education? Have you gotten a job? Do you volunteer? Have you raised a son as a single parent, working out *his* educational, medical and other daily needs? Do you own a house? Do you use a bank? Do you have friends? Do you do anything socially? Do you exercise? Do you have any political views? Do you eat?"

"I guess I *have* made other decisions," she said.

"Probably millions." I paused. "Were these all bad?"

She thought for a moment and said, "Some bad and some good."

I asked Jane to tell me about some good decisions in her life, and she recalled raising her son and some of the challenges she navigated during his younger years around learning problems and anger issues.

Then I asked, "Why do you think the three big mistakes over-shadow all of the rest, as if you did nothing but these three things in your whole life?"

Jane was so close to the chaos of anxiety obsessing about her "Big Three" that I had to pull her outside the fray and ask her to bear witness to her own life. From this perspective she could see that she wasn't incompetent. Soon, we were even able to look at her mistakes and appreciate how she rectified each one over the years. I asked her what this says about her.

"I am accountable. I take responsibility," she said. Jane's attitude about herself turned upside down and her anxiety went away.

In life, we win some and we lose some. Sometimes, we watch other people get what we haven't got, and other times it's us that people are watching. Even loss isn't permanent. Objects, opportunities and people have a way of coming back to you — in some form or another. When you're open and trusting, you won't miss them when they come.

Anxiety points out your deficits and has you saying, "I can't." When you say this a lot, you start to believe it. Even changing your language can make a big difference. "I haven't done it yet, but it's possible." Or in Jane's case, "I've done it before, so it is possible."

Take action

Have decisions been hard for you to make? Do you tend to worry that you can't trust yourself?

Write a list of some good decisions you've made in your life. Big and small.

Then, add what these actions/decisions say about you as a person.

Example: *I started the dinner in the Crock-Pot in the morning. I'm responsible and organized.*

_____

_____

_____

_____

_____

_____

_____

Trick #11: Anxiety Cuts You Down

Anxiety makes it hard to respect or like yourself very much. If you think you're not good enough, smart enough or strong enough without anxiety present, this opinion worsens once worry starts. You become a victim of your own negative thoughts about yourself and these thoughts seem so true. If you believe you're definitely inadequate and can't do anything about it, you feel powerless, which makes life seem pretty scary.

Growing up, I learned to value "humility." I thought it meant that being selfless and modest were righteous, while self-assurance and confidence were egotistical and sinful. To me, unworthiness was not only correct, but it was holy. Celebrating my accomplishments was showy, so I hid my accomplishments from the world. In doing so, I hid them from myself, too. I put my light under a veil. Too ashamed to be awesome, I'd have to counter any positive thoughts about myself with some put-downs to stay a decent person. I wanted to be good, but I wasn't supposed to be good. _Or maybe I was supposed to be good, but not think of myself as good?_ I didn't know exactly how I was supposed to be, so I had to be extra-good and self-deprecating to make sure I got it right.

In social work school, I learned to help my clients have good self-esteem. So many of them didn't feel good about themselves. It was my job to teach them how to soothe and care for themselves. This contradicted what I understood growing up about how we're supposed to see ourselves. I settled my confusion about this contradiction by illogically deciding that everyone else deserved to like themselves, but I "had a good life," and so I wasn't worthy of it.

For some of you, the sense of unworthiness runs deep and has done so for a long time. It comes from growing up in an insecure environment, from cultural expectations and from abusive voices in the past. It may be the voice of someone who should have been trustworthy — a parent, an uncle or grandparent, perhaps — but instead this person told you that you were stupid and worthless, in speech and in action, every chance they got. That voice stays with you, because you were called these names so many times that you believed them. Culture supports your negative self-view, because the ideal standards you measure yourself against are outrageous — skinny, perfect, young and genius, for instance. Instead you conclude you're a loser, disgusting, imperfect, and undeserving, and you blame yourself for being that way.

It is a strange thing people do, blame themselves when people abuse them, but they do so because it is the quickest way to make sense of the abuse. What's worse is that this blame is compounded with feeling unworthy of forgiveness.

Deva

Deva, at the age of eight, survived gang abuse similar to another client who had been tortured in a Bosnian prison camp. It was unimaginable what she endured. She was sexually abused during hazing rituals, repeatedly punched in the stomach by boys twice her age and regularly held down with a pistol at her temple while they played Russian Roulette.

Her shame was so great that it took her two years to tell me about this time in her history. Deva was steadfast that she didn't deserve to be forgiven for allowing her young self to be abused (her single mother drank heavily and Deva, with no parental guidance, did pretty much as she wanted). She hated herself with a great passion.

My heart broke. Through my eyes, she was kindhearted, whimsical, fun, creative and loyal with amazing potential. Through hers, she was disgusting, fat and unbearable.

I had to break down her walls from the outside in. I asked her how does someone "become deserving" of forgiveness? This stumped her. She spoke about remorse. To compare, she told a story of a terrorist killing many people and then feeling remorse. She said *he* was worthy of forgiveness.

Curious, I said, "You would forgive that, but not yourself?

Now she wasn't herself anymore, but an observer to herself. From this position her non-forgiveness was as absurd as I thought it was.

She smiled and quoted her mother to me (who was ten years into her recovery).

"My mother says, 'If God can forgive me, I must be able to forgive myself, because what? Do I think I am better than God?'"

Deva was able to let go of the responsibility of being abused and found compassion for herself and all she went through. Over a few weeks, we listed her survival skills and what these said about what was important to her. She began to take on these new identities and, now that she didn't hate herself, Deva began to understand that she was someone who could be counted on.

You must believe that you're worthy of healing — or you can't take another step. In Chapter Two, I wrote about the importance in my journey of changing my unworthiness to worthiness. It was only when I stopped negatively judging myself as unworthy, weak, sinful and stupid, and started having compassion for myself, that my anxiety went away.

I learned so much since my youth (thank goodness!). Confidence doesn't mean I'm egotistical. It means that I recognize my skills and trust that I'm supported. Judgments aren't at all "holy."

Holiness lifts me up, while negative self-judgment throws me in the gutter and rubs my face in the mud. Most important, I learned that I don't have to choose between being good to myself and being good to others. I can be good to both at the same time.

Judgments are a problem — and judgments *about* a problem are a worse problem. And they keep you attached to that problem. If you let go of negative self-judgments, you can stand in your confidence. You heal faster and easier than you ever thought was possible.

I still value humility, but I see it a new way. To me, humility is not having to figure it all out, not needing to have the answers or meet crazy high expectations. Humility is being free from judgments.

Take action

What negative self-judgments has anxiety been trying to get you to believe?

_____

_____

_____

_____

_____

Trick #12: Anxiety Tries to Confuse You

Anxiety tries to confuse you in order to weaken your resolve or cloud your perception. It's all part of anxiety's plot to keep you so occupied with confusion that you've no energy left to overcome it.

Christopher wrote to me on Facebook.

Hi Jodi,

My name is Christopher and I have been living with anxiety for twenty years and I am thirty-seven years old now and I am sick of it. During school, I was in a special education class since the 5th grade. Also, I was very quiet and very reserved. I do not know what you call my anxiety? It's seem like my anxiety pretty much centers around communication.

I have episodes and they vary including: my mind going blank, thinking "how much is too much," not feeling like I can follow a conversation or get all the details, not comprehending what I read, and so forth.

My counselor says (and I think you do too) that I have to "accept my anxiety and let it go"? Does that mean I have to accept all of the above? My anxiety will start to get smaller and smaller and go away?

It just seems very odd to me. I look forward to your answer.

Thanks. Christopher

P.S. My counselor says those are all irrational thinking patterns!

P.S.S. I also used to beat myself up a lot and still do from time to time. Unfortunately the mental health system has sometimes increased people's anxiety by having so many contradictory opinions about it. People are told that they are "wired this way" and will "have it forever"— the worst news you can give someone with anxiety — but then are judged when they don't get better. People are given conflicting messages that they have to "learn to live with it," and that they have to "just get their mind off of it."

Learning to live with it takes focus and effort; how can anyone do that while getting their mind off of it?

The people being served by these professionals are already having a tough time concentrating on tasks at hand, because anxiety and desperation are monopolizing their attention. Adrenaline and cortisol cause a large number of thoughts to be fired into the brain all at once. People become overwhelmed by their thoughts and then confused about which idea, path or action will make them feel better or worse.

They wish they could just take a break from worrying for a moment, but then *worry* that not being alert would leave them more vulnerable. Anxiety used to do this to me. When I conquered one of anxiety's tactics, it tried something new. These near-constant redirects of my attention kept me confused. I wasn't sure whether to face my fears or distract myself. I wasn't sure if my anxiety was a premonition something bad would happen or just an overreaction. Everything seemed right and yet, everything seemed wrong. When I blocked anxiety from the front, because it was ridiculous, it would sneak in the back door, sounding rational and smart.

My brain was running with thoughts so rapid that I'd barely have the concentration I needed to think myself out of it. The confusion consumed my brain space, and I had to work really hard on distracting myself. I was still getting over my anxiety when my kids were very little, and this confusion saw me lose my patience on more than one occasion. I felt like such a bad mom.

Once, I was panicking in the middle of a transcontinental flight. My girlfriend, attempting to distract me, asked me what I might serve for dinner if some of our friends came over the next week. My emotions were so intense I remember the conversation like it was yesterday. It took me several moments to comprehend her question. I remember seeing the words floating in my mind as I was trying to grab them. To make matters worse, getting the question turned out to be easier than coming up with an answer. In that overwhelmed state, anxiety's voice was a loud megaphone for my attention. My skills were almost drowned out. We were forced to switch tactics. She held my hand as I turned to listening to an audiobook. I couldn't follow the story, but I could focus on the voice, her hand and my breath.

It feels so powerless not being able to focus enough to follow the conversation. So when I read Christopher's comment, I could relate.

Dear Christopher,

I understand why you think it is odd to "accept" something that has been hurting you. It doesn't make sense. Logically, it seems like if you "accept" it, it means that you have to continue suffering, right? Or, "Figure out how to live with it." Then, you wonder, "Where does the letting go come in?" They contradict.

Words represent something, and sometimes they represent more than one thing. Acceptance means "the action of consenting to receive or undertake something offered."

Some traditional mental health professionals have talked about accepting, meaning "learn how to live with it." But there are many problems with this notion since it creates an internal conflict, causes confusion and, as I have experienced, makes the symptoms worse.

Your counselor may be using the word acceptance in a Buddhist way. I say this because he mentions "letting go." In this way, "accepting it" is like accepting a guest with curiosity and no judgment. (Non-judgment is key for you, as I already hear judgments perpetuating your anxious thoughts, i.e., "How much is too much?")

An example is, if you are feeling angry, you "accept" Anger by inviting it for a cup of tea. "Hello Anger, how are you? What do you want/need from me today?"

Thinking of it this way changes the relationship you have with it. It not only empowers you, but undermines the power of Anger. You have compassion instead of judgment, and this makes all the difference to how you will move through the emotion and out the other side. With non-judgment there is no work to letting go, it happens automatically.

You see, Anger, Anxiety, and many other feelings that we have, get their power from judgment (beating yourself up) and from us being afraid of them. "Acceptance," in this metaphorical context, means suspending all judgment and bringing aware-ness in — as if you are observing it for the first time. This will give you a new perspective that may invite clarity as to what you can do next. Or, it may deflate the whole problem. (This is what I mean by getting smaller and smaller.)

You'll be less confused because you don't have to figure out the answers, you can be humble and curious, and allow the answers to come to you.

Hope this helps!

Much love on your journey,

Jodi

If you thought of confusion as just a tactic of anxiety rather than evidence that you were losing it, or were stupid and crazy, would that be easier to bear? Absolutely! If you're feeling confused, stop trying to figure anything out. Don't judge yourself. Focus on decreasing your stress hormones first and foremost. This will take your task at hand from monumental to doable.

Take action

Try something today. Take a walk to burn off nervous energy or do something relaxing to increase your GABA. (GABA is the hormone that puts the brakes on the stress hormones.) Get something small to focus on like a candle flame, music or the sounds of nature. Take a shower, soak in a tub, give yourself a massage and get some rest.

While distraction by doing something is great to ward off anxiety, you also want to include in your repertoire activities that slow you down. Don't look at these activities as risky — having a blank mind vulnerable to anxiety. See them as giving your brain something easy and relaxing to focus on to help your body recover from constant stress.

Once you feel more calm and clearer, find something creative and enjoyable to take your attention.

Trick #13: Anxiety Disguises Itself

The greatest trick the Devil ever pulled
was convincing the world he didn't exist...
~Verbal, *The Usual Suspects*

One of anxiety's sneakiest tactics is to convince you that it is you. Anxiety wants you to think it's a core part of your identity, that you're just wired this way or that it comes from your DNA. Both of these tactics disempower you. These notions are supported by our culture, our families and even medical professionals, who also think of anxiety this way. It's so solidly believed that it's hard to separate this out as a tactic of anxiety. The anxiety itself becomes an excuse or a reason why "you are the way you are."

You think:

I know that I can't do it.

I am fat.

I don't like change.

I can't drive without getting a panic attack.

I'm too sensitive.

I'm not ready.

Can you see how this works in anxiety's favor? If *you can't* is true, then how will you be able to begin feeling better? It's easy to believe these things about yourself when you're thinking that you are anxiety. "I'm not good enough" is a definitive fact with no flexibility to exist differently. You're doomed to be anxious forever.

Many of my clients come to see me for problems other than anxiety and in just telling me about themselves, reveal they *had* anxiety and are on anti-depressants (SSRIs — selective serotonin re-uptake inhibitors) to control it. They explain their brain is an anxious brain and they need the medicine like diabetics need insulin. This defense signals to me that my client is weary of being judged for having anxiety and for taking any medication.

The diabetes comparison was created by pharmaceutical companies who want people to think that it's simply black and white. *You have an illness, SSRIs are the (only) way to help it.* The other pharmaceutical catch-phrase similar to this is, *You have a chemical imbalance, you can't help it.* One intention is to ease self-blame and I appreciate this. But, this statement is not true and dismisses your agency and efforts. "Imbalance" implies there are two opposing hormones — feeling good ones and feeling bad ones — that increase and decrease outside our control like they're on a single pulley system. But that's not how our brain works. The chemicals in our brain are always shifting and changing with every physical context, ingestion, feeling and emotion.

I applaud denouncing the stigma of mental illness, and I gratefully honor psychotropic medicine as a significant tool to emotional health. It saves peoples' lives every day. I advocate for prescriptions, when they can be helpful, knowing they are one of many ways to heal.

Aside from that, I worry this diabetes comparison increases the very thing it was created to alleviate, because it disempowers people, causing them to believe they have "no control over an illness that is and will always be in their brain."

With diabetes, you could decrease your sugar levels with exercise, relaxation and eating right, but if your body doesn't make any insulin at all (Type 1 Diabetes) you will always have to inject yourself with some. Anxiety and depression are different. You can increase your serotonin, tryptophan and endorphins with many different practices and by continuing those practices, you can keep them nourished and abundant.

I propose we can get rid of the stigma by reminding people how easy and common it is to get carried away by anxiety since it has all these dang tricks. It's intense and feels awful. No wonder we learn to be afraid of it. It's only when this compassion validates the person they can let any stigma or shame go. Then they land on solid ground and can step back, see the situation from a larger perspective and feel strong enough to find a way out.

What is happening?
I am feeling anxious right now. It comes and goes. It seems to be triggered by such and such... Sometimes I feel better.

Why do I feel this way?
I am overtired. I haven't been eating well. I'm going

*through a hard time. Really doubting myself lately. A rela-
tionship is going bad. I have been really stressed at work.*

What skills do I have to help myself?
*Talking to a friend. Getting distracted. Getting enough
sleep. Decreasing the stressors in my life.*

If you take away one nugget from this book, I hope it's the understanding that anxiety is not you. It never was you. It will never be you. It affects you, influences you, scares you. It affects your physical feelings and tries to control you, but it is not you. Anxiety *acts on* you. And there are things you can do to stop it.

I've never met anyone whose anxiety has a hold of them one hundred percent. You're always in there somewhere, consciously trying to do something. You are an individual, more brave and courageous than you probably realize. You have survived despite the anxiety terrorizing your life. And that's nothing short of amazing.

Anxiety also disguises itself as laziness, discomfort, protection, anger, impatience, disinterest, annoyance and stubbornness. When you think anxiety is something other than what it is, how can you address it full-on? After reading this book and especially after this chapter, you'll be able to recognize anxiety and do something about it.

Take action

How does your anxiety disguise itself?

_____

_____

_____

_____

_____

_____

_____

Trick #14: Anxiety Doesn't Want You to Talk About It

Tyler

Tyler came to my office one morning, huddling behind his mother, Jen. He was a quiet nine-year-old with downcast eyes. I invited them to have a seat in my office to see how I could help.

Jen was really worried about Tyler. They had been struggling every morning before the school bus came, when Tyler would get stomachaches and make excuses why he couldn't go. "He says, 'I have a sore throat.' Or 'I think I should stay home, I may throw up today.' I don't know what to do.

I'm wondering if there's something going on at school, but he won't tell us anything. He just says, 'Nothing.'"

Watching your children struggle with anxiety is heartbreaking for parents who feel helpless, especially if they can't put their finger on the problem — anxiety makes it very hard to determine what's wrong since it's always changing tactics and disguising itself.

Tyler had yet to admit that he was _afraid_ of anything, but hearing Jen describe his history, it occurred to me that he might be. My biggest clue proved to be that he had other worries in his life that made it hard for him to try new things. And he performed patterns before going to bed, for example touching all the corners of the windows to make sure they were shut and locked, then doing the same with his dresser to make sure the drawers were closed tightly.

I began asking him questions about his day in an attempt to discover which part may be the object, if any, of his fears. Tyler wasn't forthcoming. Undaunted, I plowed ahead. Anxiety doesn't like to be talked about directly, so I tried an indirect route.

"Is it hard to talk about or think about what stresses you about your day?"

No answer came, but I wasn't expecting one. I wanted that to sink in.

"Are you afraid of what might happen, if you did talk about it? Does it worry you what people would think?"

He looked at me. If someone is struggling to find a description for a feeling or meaning, it's helpful to give suggestions. If the description fits, it will open the person up to talk. If the description doesn't match what a person feels, it triggers the mind to think of words to describe what it *does* feel like.

"Yes," was all Tyler could say.

It was enough to tell me that I was on the right track. "What would happen if you told me? Do you worry that you'll feel worse than you do now?"

"Yes."

Anxiety tells you that if you say what you're thinking out loud, it will overwhelm you. If you speak about your fears or even think about them too much, the fears will encompass and trap you further. So you try to run away and avoid thinking about your fears or seeing those negative images in your head. You barely stay one step ahead with a growing terror they'll catch up. This avoidance sustains the fear of anxiety and so it feeds it. Worries don't like to be talked about, because isolated inside your head without witnesses to reassure you, they are very powerful.

Tyler was afraid of something *and* he was afraid of being afraid of it. There are layers of fear. I started breaking down the outer layer first.

"I know a lot of people who didn't like to talk about worries, because they were afraid their worry would eat them up whole. But once they were able to say it out loud, they felt so much better. Plus, if we knew what you were worried about, maybe we could help?" I said to Tyler.

I kept talking around the fear until we got closer. Finally, we discovered that he was terrified of going to the bus stop. It took even longer to learn why — he worried that a ghost car was going to swoop down out of thin air and kidnap him from the street corner.

Once he finally told us this, he started laughing. Sometimes when you name something out loud, it releases the energy. You can laugh, if the fear seems ridiculous. We giggled with him and made some more jokes about the ghost car at fear's expense in ways that Tyler could appreciate.

It was like a load lifted off of him and his worries about the bus stop almost completely disappeared. After Tyler expressed his fear, we didn't have any more work to do.

Paul

Paul experienced horrible abuse when he was very young. Every few months or so, the bad energy from an experience or a memory would threaten to come out. He experienced this many times in his life and after a few days of trying to hold it down, he would go out to his favorite tree and let the energy of the memory come up and out by allowing the memory to come into his consciousness. Sitting with his back rested against the bark, he'd cry for about a half hour. Afterwards he would experience great relief.

However, each time a new traumatic memory would start to niggle him, he froze with terror, pushing it down again, trying to run away and do anything to avoid it coming up and out. Each time he was afraid that, this time, it would take him over completely — he'd become permanently insane — if he let it loose. But it never did; he released it near the tree again and his anxiety evaporated.

Anxiety told Paul and Tyler that if they let it out they would feel worse, because anxiety knows that letting it out would be the end of its control.

Humans tend to be really scared of experiencing feelings. This can make us avoid them at all costs. But the feelings affect you negatively anyway. Here again, in the guise of protecting you, your anxiety convinces you that by avoiding your feelings, it's keeping you from suffering.[20]

I've found that when you allow yourself to feel, release and talk about your worries, you're relieved and the feelings subside. Inside your head, things are much more powerful than they are when you let them out. It's never as bad as you think to say things out loud. The stress of holding things in can be awful.

Take action

Write down your worst fears. Next to it put a number between 1 and 10 representing how likely it is to happen, with 10 being "It's absolutely likely." Then, decide how much time and energy it's worth.

Worst fear 1-10   Worth it? Y or N

_____   _____   _____

_____   _____   _____

_____   _____   _____

---

20   Check out my "Allow Yourself to Feel" video at jodiaman.com/you1anxiety0

_____   _____   _____

_____   _____   _____

_____   _____   _____

_____   _____   _____

_____   _____   _____

_____   _____   _____

_____   _____   _____

Trick #15: Anxiety Tells You, "You Can't Handle It"

Last, but not least, telling you that you can't handle an event, a possibility, an opportunity, a hardship, a social event or life in general is the most powerful tactic that anxiety uses on every sufferer.

The belief that you can't handle something is a common trigger for your anxiety. Many things seem to initiate the sympathetic response (the fight or flight reaction). A sound, sight, smell or sensation that reminds you of a past trauma, a perceived fear or the anticipation of a perceived fear, such as heights or knowing that you have to sleep alone when your partner is out of town. Perhaps a physical sensation like nausea or an emotion like feeling overwhelmed, guilty or embarrassed.

However, what invariably happens between the stimuli and the anxiety is a fleeting thought, one that you hardly realize you're having as it crosses your mind. This is anxiety's trigger.

Oh, no! I think I'm going to get anxious right now!

Oh, no! Here it comes.

Oh, no! What if I get anxious right now? I can't handle it.

You're afraid of how the panic feels and that you can't handle that awful feeling. (Remember, anxiety is the leftover sympathetic nervous response and accompanying rapid, negative and scary thoughts when you're not in physical danger.)

If you weren't afraid of handling the fear, it would just fizzle out. If you thought, *I might panic, but cool beans!*, it wouldn't come. If you said, *Bring it on!*, it would stop the panic attack instantly. Anxiety needs you to be afraid in order to sustain the biological fear response. (See Trick #8.)

If you've experienced panic, know how horrible it feels and you're afraid of it coming, you fear it will take your sanity as its prisoner, just like I did — just like almost everyone else that I talk to about it. You feel stripped of your abilities and your confidence to "handle it." The fear infiltrates your very identity (Trick #13), taking over who you are, making you forget everything that you know about yourself and the world (Trick #7).

The fear that you can't handle it brings all the tricks together into one: Fear becomes your body clock as you lose many minutes, hours, and sometimes days to anxiety's control. You can't stop it. You're powerless against the agonizing discomfort, you're frantic for relief from its torments. All because you think, *Oh, no, I can't handle this!*

You become anxiety and lose yourself.

When I was young, I thought about going into politics. I thought it was a good way to change the world. When my anxiety was at its worst, I watched politicians on the news respond to world tragedies and I decided that I couldn't do it. That was my only reason. I wasn't fazed by the criticisms I'd open myself up to as a public figure. I was confident I could withstand any temptation to become corrupt and self-serving. However, what scared me to my core was thinking that I'd have to be poised in the midst of devastation and war, and I didn't think I could handle that. I figured I would be panicked and out of control during those times and unable to talk to a friend, let alone reassure a whole nation on live TV. I was more scared of handling the panic than the tragedy.

Same with death. Growing up, I was afraid of death. As I got older I made peace with it, but was confused that I was still anxious when thinking about the act of dying. Partly this is an unavoidable biological issue. Responding to any threat to life is the specific point of the sympathetic response. What I finally realized was that I was more afraid of handling anxiety *while* I was dying, than I was about dying. It makes sense that I thought I couldn't handle anxiety, since it felt so out of control and horrible. But once I learned that I could handle it, it *wasn't* so out of control or horrible. It just wasn't…there.

When I was pregnant with my daughter, my anxiety increased again. This is understandable, as I had morning sickness twenty-four hours a day. I went to an energy healer to help ease my nausea. Later that night I had a panic attack. I freaked out and drove back to him the next day, desperate to feel better again.

He put his hand on mine, looked into my panicked eyes and said, "You just have to trust yourself."

This advice was pivotal in my healing. It was the first time I noticed the inverse relationship between trust and anxiety. I hadn't realized I didn't trust myself and that was the problem. When I trusted myself to handle situations, the anxiety didn't come. When I didn't, it did. This gave me something to focus my attention on, building trust in myself.

Take action

Watch my video *How to Deal with Anxiety and Trust Issues* on YouTube. (Subscribe while you are there!)

It's important to understand these *Tricks and Tactics of Anxiety.* Knowing them and naming them will help you see them a mile away.

Remember, when you're too close to the chaos of your problems, it's hard to get any perspective to feel better. Getting distance and recognizing that they're tricks and lies can help you respond to them differently and with a whole lot less suffering.

Take action

Practice what you learned. Below is a list of thoughts that you might have. Some are examples of the anxiety talking, and some are examples of your wisdom. See if you can notice the difference. Circle the thoughts that are your wisdom. Put a line through anxiety's lies.

I can't do this.

I always get hurt in relationships.

I'm different from everyone else.

Oh, no, I might panic right now.

I'll just get out of bed. I may feel better.

I can't eat.

I should take a walk.

Breathe.

This is not going to work.

I can't go. Something bad will happen.

I can't handle this. It's not worth even trying.

There's Sally. I can stand near her.

Oh, no, I'm going to panic! I have to get out of here.

I'll call Cindy. She'll help me feel better.

I won't worry about getting it all done. I'll just begin.

It's going to be okay.

I'm not okay!

I'm weak.

I'm alone.

I'm not alone, and I've done it before!

When the thoughts are from someone else's head they're easier to sort out. They may not be so easy in your own mind. Now it's your turn — write the phrases anxiety uses on you.

_____

_____

_____

_____

_____

_____

_____

_____

Now write down some of the confident things you say to debunk anxiety and help calm yourself down.

_____

_____

_____

_____

_____

Writing your thoughts out on paper will give you the distance you need to see them outside of yourself. This will help you distinguish between you and anxiety. This would be a big step forward in feeling better.

Anxiety uses whatever it can to throw you off balance. It doesn't care about you. It will apparently stop at nothing — except that it *will*. It *will* stop at your self-confidence, it will stop at you knowing that you can handle anxiety and it will stop at you trusting yourself. You have much more control than you think when anxiety is present. It's time to uncover and breathe life into your skills.

Making Your Comeback: Your Skills and Knowledges

Your Personal Invitation to Heal

You are cordially invited to heal from past and present hurts. They happened, but that was then and this is now. They don't have to define you.

You are invited to let go of worries because you know that you can handle whatever comes your way. The risk of "going for it" is that you have an experience you can grow from. You can gain confidence in your skills in managing yourself. You can be proud of your response.

You are respectfully invited to connect with people, to see relationships and situations from the big picture where things are not so personal and not as "against you" as you thought. You will see that everyone is going through their own stuff.

You are invited to stop taking yourself so seriously. Ease up. Relax.

You are invited to breathe easy since no matter what situation you are in, you are not alone.

You are invited to have more fun, more silliness, more love.
You are invited to shine.

~RSVP to jodiaman.com
(*Print this from jodiaman.com/invitation)

Do you feel like you've shaken off some chains in the last chapter? I hope so. Now it's time to live freely! This is your time to shine through all of that fear and be the person you're supposed to be in the world.

By deconstructing the anxiety, it can no longer block you from going forward. If you *still* feel blocked and trapped, Chapter Four will be there for you to go through again. You can see if there is anything left that the fear is telling you to believe that you still think is *right or real*. If so, break that down, too. Grab it from the outside and take it apart layer by layer until you can see clearly.

Otherwise, keep reading from here, because I might explain something a different way that can help you move forward.

You've deflated the power of anxiety by getting inside its mind and figuring out how it works on you. Now that doubt and anxiety aren't obstacles in the way, you can see your skills and connect with them. You can use them as you see fit to move swiftly and easily through your life. Even if you think you have no skills — you do. You are *very* skilled! Anxiety tries to make them invisible, but you couldn't have gotten this far in life without using a lot of them.

As an agent in your life, you control how you respond to experiences, how you think about an event, what you decide to do and how you act in response to what happens to you. This response defines the differences in your emotional well-being, your self-confidence, and how you read the world. In the simplest terms, in how happy you are.

So let's look at the skills, learn more from others going through the same things, and hone what you have so that you're on the way to a happier life. A life you can enjoy without anything to hold you back.

The Most Common Skills and Knowledges

Here are fifteen skills and knowledges that have emerged as frequently helpful to people and families I've worked with. These are real examples of the skills people possess. I'm sure you've already used some or all of them yourself.

1. Face Your Fears
2. Be Flexible
3. Ask Questions
4. See the Big Picture
5. Know Things Are Transient
6. Connect
7. Find a Higher Priority
8. Practice Exposure
9. Harry Potter It
10. Nourish Yourself
11. Believe You Can
12. Lighten Up
13. Talk About It
14. Ask It to Come
15. Remember What You Know

Skill #1: Face Your Fears

Do the thing you fear most and
the death of fear is certain.

~Mark Twain

Celia

Celia felt a strong desire to tell her husband that she loved him and that he was important to her — except this evoked intense anxiety. So much so that she froze each time she tried and delayed it for years. Every day she thought, *Today, I'll do it,* but her anxiety would psych her out of it again, saying she wasn't ready. At the same time, Celia was confused by how intense her anxiety became, because she knew he would love hearing it.

Celia's anxiety was evasive. It had her dreading telling him without being clear on what exactly frightened her. It was so intense that she didn't question it, leaving her stuck in the chaos and unable to see any other perspective.

Since her anxiety was a barrier, I wanted to understand *what* was worrying about telling him, so we could get it out of the way. I used a simple question to get Celia the distance to become a witness to her anxiety.

"What will happen, if you tell him?"

Celia pictured the situation as if she was watching the scenario play out in front of her — little characters of herself telling him. She explained her husband's response was positive.

Because she was now speaking outside her anxiety's influence, I could ask her to clarify the fear. "What are you afraid of happening, then?"

"Nothing. I guess I'm afraid of being vulnerable while I tell him."

Now we knew what we were dealing with. Looking into this fear, we discovered that in her past, Celia was taught that you could be attacked when you're vulnerable. If she opened her heart, the amygdala would trigger a sympathetic nervous system response, because there's a body memory of this being linked with danger. To keep her anxiety at bay, she'd been avoiding vulnerability. This was having negative effects on her relationship, because it created a barrier to intimacy.

"Vulnerability is not dangerous, being vulnerable with danger around is dangerous," I said.

Celia trusted her husband not to attack her, if she shared her feelings. So, she was able to set aside the fear of vulnerability in this context where there was no danger. She called him as soon as she left my office and said, "I want you to know that you mean the world to me."

She only needed to break the ice. That night they talked and she spoke aloud all of the compliments and gratitude she'd been wanting to share. It was just as wonderful as she imagined.

The quickest way to get rid of a fear of doing something — speaking in public, driving over a bridge, going to restaurants, going to school, being close to someone — is to do it. Even though facing your fear is anxiety-provoking, it's worthwhile. It's after you've done it that the magic happens. Your fear response energy is used up by the action. You realize that you've survived, which builds confidence.

Then, in doing it again and again you further increase your confidence and the action becomes familiar. It's hard to think you can't handle it or will go off an insanity cliff once you've done it several times. Anxiety is debunked, has no power and ceases being attached to that action.

By doing it, you are also retraining your amygdala. While you were still afraid, that action — and even *thinking* about that action — triggered your fear response. When you do it over and over and aren't physically or emotionally threatened, your amygdala no longer categorizes that memory as dangerous, and it stops setting off the response. In the movie *The Truman Show*, the main character, Truman grows up as the central figure in a TV show, only he doesn't know it. His family, friends and coworkers are cast members in the show, but he thinks it's real life in a small town on an island. From a young age, Truman's greatest desire is to be an explorer. This is a challenge to the director, who wants to keep Truman on set so as not to sabotage the show.

When Truman is in grade school, the writers design a boating accident where his father dies in a storm. As they hoped, Truman develops a fear of water and he doesn't step back in a boat. The director preys on that fear and controls him for almost twenty more years.

After several clues, Truman begins to get suspicious and tries to find out what's really happening. Knowing he's trapped on the island, he decides he must escape by sea. The director, frantically trying to save the show, causes a storm over his boat in attempt to scare him back to shore.

Truman is lashed by the weather. He's terrified, but determined after all this time to do what he's afraid of and stays his course. In the most powerful part of the movie, Truman's tenacity takes over. He yells, "Is that the best you can do?"

The director intensifies the storm in one last attempt to get Truman to back down, but instead Truman becomes more empowered. Fear loses its grip. The storm ends. The director has no more power and allows Truman to be free.

Anxiety will do the same. Stand up, face your fear and say, "Give me the best you've got! I am not afraid of you!"

Then watch anxiety slink away with its tail between its legs.

Doing something unfamiliar takes gumption. Doing something you're afraid of takes outright courage. Anxiety may have been talking you out of something for years. If you wait until you are "ready" or "not afraid anymore," you'll be waiting for a long time. Being *ready*, you think, is when your mind is feeling so perfectly confident that you won't feel anxious. However, you won't ever have a guarantee that you won't feel anxious so, unfortunately, not being *ready* becomes a reason to not try. It's a powerful excuse to stay stuck.

You will feel ready and not afraid *after* you've done it. If your fear is great, you can try doing something small and gradually increase the difficulty to make the transition easier. Many people tell me they've worried about doing things in the past, but not any longer. Almost invariably they explain it's because they did the activity and it went okay. Confidence is gained after you do something.

A small amount of confidence can be enough to help you try something in the first place. That's why, like with Celia, I unpack the anxiety first. But other times, people tell me accounts of finally doing something that they've been afraid of doing, saying, "I just did it before I could think about it." It wasn't that they had more confidence. It was that they didn't take the time to allow the fear to talk them out of it. Hesitation gives the anxiety time to spiral.

When you try something that frightens you, the activity is not nearly as bad as you thought it was going to be. The fear is the problem more than the activity itself. And you'll feel a rush of pride when you accomplish it. That pride gives you the energy and confidence to try again. With familiarity, new memories and associations develop around the activity, leaving no room for the fear.

Running away from fear gives the anxiety power. When you let it know you're afraid, it can spiral into a greater intensity. Anxiety has no power unless you're afraid of it. Trust yourself. Face it, feel it and watch it pass.

Ready or not, make yourself ready and just try it!

Take action

List times in your life where you waited to be ready, but that time never came (e.g., a high school crush you wanted to talk to, but graduation came and went before you worked up the courage).

_____

_____

_____

_____

_____

_____

_____

Identify some times when you were forced to face your fears due to circumstances beyond your control (having to conquer your fear of heights to rescue your cat).

_____

_____

_____

_____

_____

_____

Skill #2: Be Flexible

A tree growing in a forest can have a hard time getting to the sunlight through the canopy, and so they become flexible. They do what they need to do, bend and twist, to reach the pockets of light coming through other branches.

Anxiety wants you to be unbendable. It uses black and white thinking (Trick #2) making you think that you need something to be a certain way, *or else*. When things don't happen that certain way, anxiety has you all up in arms, tied in knots, fumbling, immobilized and discombobulated. When things vary from the plan, anxiety can come in and come in heavy. You think that you can't handle it.

Things change all the time. Rarely does anything ever go as planned. Anxiety uses change to convince you into thinking that you've failed, you're inadequate and you can't handle it. None of those thoughts is true.

You've handled a change in plans before.

If you expect one thing and something else happens, it's not necessarily bad. Changes can be benign, good or even fantastic. People who believe they are not good at change see *all* change as a threat to security, but it isn't. Humans are extremely adaptable creatures. We have amazing problem-solving skills. When initial expectations are not met, we adjust. When your mind gets caught up in looking for solutions, you'll prevent it from being immobilized by panic.

Jamie

Jamie was telling me that she didn't want her ex-husband to introduce his new girlfriend to their six-year-old daughter.

"She has a big reaction to change. She can't handle it. That's why I've kept this big house and stayed in town where I don't feel like I belong. Changing schools took a long transition. Talk of moving overwhelmed her and even last year, when my car's lease was up, I was thinking out aloud about trading it in and she burst into tears. I'm afraid she won't be able to handle it."

I asked Jamie, "With each of those examples, there is an object of loss. Is change the problem or is it losing something she loves that she grieves?"

Whether or not we are aware of it, this six-year-old, her mother, you and I all manage and handle change constantly. If the pants you want to wear are dirty, you pick another pair. There are no more apples, so you find something else to snack on. You can't do something on your computer, and you Google how to do it. Your friend texts you that she's running late for your coffee date, so you check your email while you wait. You figure it out.

When life circumstances have people feeling out of control, there's a tendency to become more rigid emotionally and physically as they attempt to regain control. My daughter broke her dominant hand recently. The first month following the injury, she needed us to scribe her schoolwork. In the beginning this was anxiety-provoking, because she concentrated on what she couldn't change — not being able to write by herself, missing classwork and assignments due to doctor appointments and feeling trapped in her cast. She felt totally out of control and in an attempt to right her world, she became strict about the order of her homework and where she put everything. Rather than relieve her, this increased her anxiety.

Breaking a hand is not a tragedy, but this anxiety was trying for the whole family. It took her some time to let go of those laments and use her energy to problem-solve, advocate and express herself, and figure out how to do things with one hand. Afterward, we were able to look at the experience as an opportunity for her to develop her skills in being flexible. We also remarked how this will help her the next time she experiences change or challenge.

You can't count on anything to stay the same. Everything changes. You have the skills to be flexible or you wouldn't be alive today. You may believe

that you don't do well with change, but you are. When you're in the midst of change and handling it effectively, it's rare to stop and realize, "Hey, I'm handling change well right now…"

It's time to break down this belief. Ask yourself why you're afraid of change. Anxiety will tell you that change is out of control, but that's not true. Telling you to be more rigid is another way your anxiety pretends it's protecting you, but really it's causing great suffering. Being *inflexible* feels much more out of control, because your flexibility is where you *have* control. No matter what happens, you can choose how to respond.

Here are some ways to be flexible.

- Have a plan for other possibilities. Expect them, don't fear them.

- Try to see other meanings in what is happening. There are usually other ways to see this situation, other perspectives that help relieve some of the tension, anxiety and self-blame you feel.

- Get the opinion of someone you trust. Other people have the distance to see things differently than you. (Or take a step back from the experience yourself to get a different view.)

- Allow yourself to feel upset. Don't judge yourself for feeling the loss of the original plan. Self-judgment breeds more anxiety. When you allow yourself to be upset, you go through the disappointment and out the other side faster.

- Adjust your attitude. Make some lemonade with those lemons. Think of something else that would work. Use your creativity. Think of it as a challenge or an adventure.

- Trust yourself. You can handle this. You've done it before and so you can do it again. (Don't let anxiety use Trick #4:

Anxiety Insists: "This Is Real." Find something similar that you did do. Skills do transfer from one situation to another.)

- Have faith that there is a higher purpose to your experiences even if you don't see it.

Stop fighting change. It's not your enemy. You can control you, your responses, your expectations and your preferences. You can go with the flow and bend, enjoying yourself and what you can do, or you can lament your misfortunes and panic. It's your choice.

Take action

Think of an activity coming up soon.

What might possibly change? What can you do about it?

_____

_____

_____

_____

_____

_____

_____

Skill #3: Ask Questions

When anxiety uses evasiveness, curiosity is your best ally. You're smart. Anxiety is savvy and definitely a little sneaky, but it's not necessarily smart. Don't settle for what it tells you. Ask questions. Sooner or later, anxiety's logic will crumble and you'll be clear that there's nothing of substance to fear.

We're afraid of the unknown and the mysterious. When you find out more about anxiety, it can't hold that power over you. For example, physical pain is so much worse when you don't know where it comes from. Fear compounds it. Having a disease sounds terrifying, but when you ask questions to find out more about it, you understand better how to manage it. More information helps to calm your fears.

In order to find out all I could, I used this inquisitive skill with myself. Here are the questions I asked anxiety, and I demanded that it answers me.

Q: What do you want from me?

A: All of your attention so you get frozen and don't do anything to get rid of me.

Q: Why do you want to ruin my life?

A: I like hanging out in your life. I like owning you and telling you what to do. If you had a life, you wouldn't listen anymore. The less relationships you have, the more I control you.

Q: Why do you tell me that you're more powerful than me?

A: So you will believe that and don't overpower me. I know you can, but if you knew that, you might do it. That wouldn't be good for me.

Q: Why do you make me feel like I'll have to deal with you forever?

A: I would like to stay with you forever. I have a good gig going. If you think it's forever, it scares you and feeds me. All good stuff! Don't you want me forever?

Q: Why do you make me forget what I know?

A: This also gets you to listen to me. I can't have your reasoning and intelligence giving you power. If you knew those things, you'd get rid of me.

Q: Why do you make me feel powerless?

A: So I maintain power of you. If you think you're powerless, I have an easier time. When you remember that you do have power and control, that's it. I'm toast.

Q: Why do you sometimes seem to come out of the blue?

A: Your amygdala responds before your mind does. It feels out of the blue, but there's always an inner or outer context. This helps me, though. If you think I come out of the blue, then I can scare you by thinking you are never safe from me! It makes me very threatening.

Q: Why do you try to separate me from all who love me?

A: Duh! They will help you see the truth. That's not good for me. So if I make you afraid of being vulnerable, you don't stay or get close to people.

Q: How do you convince me to listen to you?

A: I'm clever. I make you think it is very important. I make you feel desperate. I make you think it would be better for you to listen. Hahaha! All lies!

Q: Why do you lie to me?

A: It's the only way you'll listen. I have to make life or the situation sound bad.

Q: Why do I believe you?

A: I'm that good.

Q: What would my life be like if I didn't fraternize with you?

A: Um, wait a minute...don't do anything rash. You need me!

Q: Why?

A: Because.

Q: Because why?

A: Because you just do, that's all.

Q: Why don't you just leave me alone?

A: You need me.

Q: Why?

A: Because.

Q: Because why?

A: Because you just do, that's all.

Now, I ask myself questions.

Q: Why do you believe the Anxiety is more powerful than you are?

Me: Because I can't see it coming. It feels so bad and I can't concentrate on anything else. It feels so real. I feel like I'm going crazy.

Q: What has made you feel powerless?

Me: It's really convincing. I doubt myself. I've been anxious so long, I'm not sure I can get over it. I may be fine for a little while, but it comes back. And I hate it so much!

Q: What skills have you used to get through hard times in the past?

Me: Distraction with something requiring loads of mental concentration and creativity, like designing something. I was really anxious when my sister-in-law asked me to design and make her bridal veil, and it helped me for several weeks thinking about that. Sometimes planning a party or having a house project. Starting my business distracted me for a long time.

Q: Why is getting rid of Anxiety so important to you?

Me: I no longer want to stay home instead of being social. I want to be there for people, if they're dealing with tragedy and death. I look forward to being able to relax with my husband. That's living. Being with anxiety is not. I want fun in my life. And joy. And relationships. Did I mention fun?

Q: What do you want to tell Anxiety?

Me: Take your lies and shove them. I'm learning all about you and I know what you are trying to do. I don't think it will work the same way now that I am on to you.

Q: When do you want to reclaim your life from Anxiety?

Me: Right now.

Q: How do you know you can do this?

Me: If anyone can do it, I can do it. I have to. I refuse to live like this. I have to get my life back. I am determined and I won't stop until I live free. I'm pretty savvy myself and I don't give up. I have hope. I have support. I eat well and exercise and get enough sleep. I can do this, because I have the tenacity to stick with it as long as it takes.

Q: Who is around that believes in you?

Me: God. My husband. My friends.

Fear comes from the unknown, so don't hesitate to ask questions and seek answers to calm your heart and mind.

Take action

It's your turn to demand answers from Anxiety for the following questions. You answer as if you are in the head of personified anxiety. What would *Anxiety* say…

What do you want from me?

_____

Why do you want to ruin my life?

_____

Why do you tell me that you're more powerful than me?

_____

Why do you make me feel like I'll have to deal with you forever?

_____

Why do you make me forget what I know?

_____

Why do you make me feel powerless?

_____

Why do you sometimes seem to come out of the blue?

_____

Why do you have me thinking that I'm weak?

_____

Why do you try to separate me from all who love me?

_____

How do you convince me to listen to you?

_____

Why do you have me focus on the worst possible scenario?

_____

Why do you lie to me?

_____

Why do I believe you?

_____

What would my life be like, if I didn't fraternize with you?

_____

Why don't you just leave me alone?

_____

Now, ask yourself these questions: Why do you believe _Anxiety_ is more powerful than you are?

What has made you feel powerless?

_____

_____

What skills have you used to get through hard times in the past?

_____

What is your biggest motivator to get rid of Anxiety?

_____

Why is that important?

_____

What do you want to tell Anxiety?

_____

When do you want to reclaim your life from Anxiety?

_____

What skills have you used in getting over Anxiety in the past?

_____

How do you know you can do this?

_____

Who is around that believes in you?

_____

_____

Skill #4: See the Big Picture

"I'm not doing well," Deva (from Trick #2) said as soon as she sat down. "I haven't been doing well for months."

This was news to me. For the last two months she'd been happier than I'd ever seen her. She smiled and was engaged with friends. Deva was having fun and feeling good about herself. All these things were quite rare up until then.

"Tell me what's happening. Things seemed to be going well this summer. When did it change?"

"I thought I was doing well, but I think this has been festering the whole time underneath. I wasn't good. I was just faking it."

This was the meaning she made. That summer, *for the first time in her life*, she felt good. Feeling depressed and anxious again after that was disheartening and confusing, but it felt real, since it was familiar. The good time — being different — felt fake and hard to hold on to. It's like when you're nauseous, you can't imagine feeling okay. Depression encompassed her and she couldn't see or understand anything outside of that story.

Life is full of ups, downs and everything in between. If each of us plotted our life history (or even a few months) on a Pleasure vs. Time graph (Figure 5.), it would zigzag all over the place. There would be little squiggles, from stubbing your toe or getting a free coffee, and tall peaks and deep troughs from promotions to a break-up. Your pleasure rating would even change within the span of one day.

When you're going through a down period, like inside the circle, you see the immediate suffering rather than the whole graph. You probably don't give two nickels about the whole graph — you're in survival mode. You have tunnel vision and can't see anything besides the decline. The lower you feel, the more this happens and the lower you feel. (Again a downward spiral.) Being depressed and anxious reminds you of all the other bad times. The good times disappear from your view.

Figure 5.

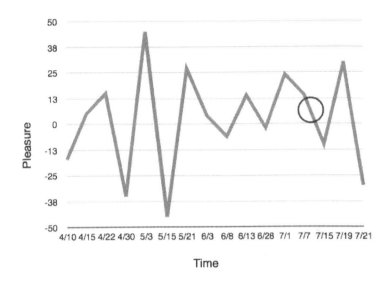

If you looked at the whole thing, the big picture, you'd notice and feel comforted that there are both ups and downs. Life doesn't seem so foreboding.

I had a young woman ask me, "How do I know if I am happy? When I'm sad, I know it. But I never know when I'm happy."

When you're sad, you're thinking, reflecting, ruminating, making meaning, trying to figure it out, defending your limitations, experiencing shame and fear, and thinking about your sad history. You are very aware of your sadness. When you're happy, instead of pondering *why*, you are distracted — busy living and doing things that create more happiness. You know when you're happy when you're not in your head all the time analyzing how you feel. Without the tunnel vision that displeasure brings, your awareness expands and this feels much more comfortable.

In previous chapters, you've heard examples of how I helped people to step outside the chaos of their situation and see from a bigger picture view. It never looks as bleak and scary from this perspective. You feel more control simply by understanding the situation better and realizing an action you can take toward the higher good. Taking that step back is an excellent skill for overcoming anxiety. Having distance from the chaos of the moment, outside that tunnel vision, changes how you make meaning and affects how you feel.

Sometimes asking big spiritual questions can help you get over your problems, because the questions help you make meaning of what happens. Here are some examples of such questions.

Why do bad things happen? Why are we here?

Not that you want difficult times to happen at all, but this is life. Difficult times come and you'll have to go through them. But within them, there are a lot of options. This is where your power is. If you are so focused on what is happening *to* you, you forget your agency. While people are going through problems, they tend to learn and grow. This doesn't mean that it's okay something bad happened or that we're glad to have suffered, but we can still appreciate what we receive from the experience.

Many people conclude this is the reason for life — to learn from our experiences.

You know this idea is common when you read quotations like these.

> *There is no such thing as a problem*
> *without a gift for you in its hands.*
> *You seek problems because you need their gifts.*
> ~Richard Bach

A ship is safe at dock,
but if it spends too long there,
the bottom rots out.

~Unknown

If you are irritated by every rub,
how will your mirror be polished?

~Rumi

Learning and growing gives meaning to our challenging times.

Marlin in the movie *Finding Nemo* is so afraid of something bad happening to Nemo that he doesn't want *anything* to happen to him.

Dory is confused.

Marlin: I promised I'd never let anything happen to him.

Dory: Hmm. That's a funny thing to promise.

Marlin: What?

Dory: Well, you can't never let anything happen to him. Then nothing would ever happen to him.

Wise words. When we experience fear, we lose sight of this big picture. The purpose of life is to live it and have experiences. Taking risks is part of living life to the fullest. Life would be pretty boring without challenges. Getting through them breeds confidence. Adventure is interesting and invigorating. There is a lot to gain. Building skills through small risks helps prepare you for when harder times come along.

When we went on vacation this summer, I knew we'd have some adventure. We were open to that and looked forward to it as part of our experience, rather than being afraid of something bad happening. I wanted my kids to struggle a little and bond over getting through it. Like Leo having a stomach virus, when we waited six hours in a hot overcrowded, smelly, third-world airport, huddled with our bags in a circle on the floor under the stairs waiting to get on a small plane headed for a bumpy flight over the sea. We were compassionate with each other, chatted with the folks around us, kept a good attitude and made it.

I'm glad my kids learned what they could get through, so harder challenges won't knock them down.

It's helpful to see life experience symbolically. Instead of being overwhelmed by panic about what terrible things could happen to me, I think of life as a learning experience. The good times, the bad times and even the anxiety are all part of it.

Thinking of anxiety as just an experience helped me immeasurably. Anxiety wasn't so real and I took it less personally. I started writing down the things I learned each day. It was like a gratitude journal (writing down five things a day that I'm grateful for), but specific to lessons I took out of my daily living experiences. Some lessons were harder than others, but they were all lessons. Thinking of them as *lessons* made them easier to handle than thinking of them as *losses*. This practice empowered me. I could see that feeling anxious wasn't the end of the world, so I was no longer dreading some terrible thing to happen. I had a distance to see anxiety in the big picture of my life, and from here I could live free from it.

Take action

Write down five things you have learned from anxiety.

_____

_____

_____

_____

_____

Committing to this as a daily practice will help you progress faster!

Skill #5: Know Things Are Transient

Danielle

Danielle is a twenty-six-year-old woman who told me she learned, "nothing was permanent" after losing a friend though a break-up. Her life was never the same after that. She decided not to get close to anyone else again for fear she would lose that person, too.

This attitude struck me as very sad, because connecting and getting close make life worth living.

I've lost friends before and I know the pain so I gave Danielle time to cry.

Then I said, "The bad news is, nothing is permanent." I paused for emphasis and added, "The good news is, nothing is permanent."

After giving it a moment to sink in, I said, "Even pain and sadness pass."

Even loss is impermanent.

Permanent means forever, and forever is an awfully long time. It's so long that *permanent* is a concept humans can barely comprehend. With our limited knowledge of the future, we can't definitively conclude the permanency of anything, yet we often feel loss as everlasting. That's a trick of anxiety. To convince us that loss is inevitable and unstoppable, and that we can't recover from it. We even choose isolation to protect ourselves from the horror of loss, but this perpetuates our suffering, not prevents it. (See Skill #6.)

Relationships can be repaired, sometimes many years later. Or you can heal that loss in your heart even if that other person is not involved. Even death is impermanent depending on what you believe. For me, there's just too much scientific documentation that consciousness[21] continues after biological death to dismiss it. Regardless, relationships continue after death. I've witnessed first-hand hundreds of people growing close, making peace, changing, ending, forgiving and rekindling relationships with their loved ones who have passed on. The fact that things change is the only certainty.

The word "attachment" used in Buddhism can be confusing. Novices to this philosophy have apprehension about detaching since they worry this means disconnecting from something they love or having to accept the permanence of loss. It feels wrong to abandon what they treasure, especially if it's a person.

They think acceptance means to believe the loss is okay, but that isn't right. Our attachment is actually to the fear of losing permanently, which just causes more fear and suffering. Non-attachment (acceptance) simply means not judging a situation as good or bad. It's just seeing it as an experience and being gentle and loving with yourself about how you feel. When you understand everything will change and keep changing, the permanency of the loss doesn't exist.

If you've lost someone in your life, I know how hurt and bereaved you feel. Grief is an expression of love. It means you loved with a passionate, open heart. You are beautiful. Love yourself through that. If they've passed away, talk to them. Ask for advice or a sign of their presence. If they're alive, you may not be speaking to each other right now, but the story is not over yet. For now, you can still connect and be one, love them from a distance and love yourself in that place, too.

When you feel loss, you're just learning a new way of being connected. You're disconnecting from one story and moving over

---

21   Bruce Greyson and Charles Flynn, *The Near-Death Experience: Problems, Prospects, Perspectives* (Springfield, Illinois: Charles C. Thomas, 1984)

to a new one about your relationship. You have control over creating that. Your stories can and are changing constantly. You can reinvent yourself and change the story every day.

I was talking a woman down from a panic attack on the phone. She was telling me what was freaking her out the most. "I'll have to live with these thoughts. I will never be okay again," she said.

This idea has got to be one of the scariest things that anxiety does. (Trick #8: Scares You) It makes you look into the future and only see it staring you down. As if they are already losses, you mourn every event in your future, confident they will be fraught with this horrible feeling. When you have made premature conclusions of failure, life feels hopeless.

When your panic is this intense, remind yourself that this is just panic, not death, not psychosis, not a cliff... and it will pass. I've worked with people with anxiety for twenty years. I coached my kids through it and also got myself over it. In all that time, I learned one thing that I can be sure of — anxiety is always changing.

Even in the course of a single day, your anxiety goes up and down. And though anxiety wouldn't like you to know this, you're controlling the intensity. It only feels like this anxiety is more intense, because it's happening right now.

This, too, shall pass. Most likely you've been here before and came out on the other side. Change is guaranteed in life. I can promise that you won't stay in this exact place forever. That would be impossible.

Take action

Reflect on your present situation and think about times in the past where you have felt a similar panic. List them here.

_____

_____

_____

_____

Now think back to how you came through these situations. Make a list of actions you took to survive them.

_____

_____

_____

_____

Skill #6: Connect

Finding the soul and connecting with other souls, even spirits can have a powerful comforting effect on those who suffer deeply.

~Lewis Mehl-Madrona, *Coyote Medicine*

Ted and I invited a bunch of friends over one summer evening. That afternoon, while we were getting our apartment ready, I began to panic. Afraid I couldn't hold it together during the party, I decided to leave (go to my mom's) for the evening and Ted hosted the *soiree* himself. I missed an awesome night of sitting on our porch sharing food and catching up with our best friends. When anxiety is high, there's a tendency to pull away from people — even safe, loving ones. There are many reasons for this. That night, my reasons were shame, embarrassment, worry the anxiety would get worse if I didn't focus on calming it, the desperation to avoid crowds and difficulty concentrating. Anxiety loved this and fed off this isolation, because that way, it kept my full attention. I didn't feel better focusing on it. I felt worse! And I missed a good time that could have given me some much needed joy.Sometimes anxiety says that you'll annoy people or burden them by being too needy, so you pull back from relationships to protect the other person. Unfortunately, shame that you're too needy intensifies your despair and longing for acknowledgement and help.

You also isolate yourself, because you worry that you'll be judged negatively by others, creating distance to protect yourself from being hurt. But, isolation contributes to unhappiness.

There are mean people in the world and judgmental people in the world. At first glance, someone's treatment of you appears to be out of your control. Soon, doubt tells you that you must have invited it in some way. Your mind searches to figure out which it is. Let me settle it. People aren't mean to you because they don't like you. They are mean to you, because they don't like *themselves*. People judging you are judging themselves ten times more.

Also, your fear about people judging you is there, because you don't believe you're good enough. You can only feel bad about negative judgment coming from another when it triggers a negative judgment you already have of yourself. If someone gave a criticism like, *You always pick the smallest shell from the bowl*, that you didn't care about nor found true in the least, you'd shrug it off as ridiculous. It wouldn't bother you. This means that if you're more kind and compassionate with yourself, you'll worry less about what other people are thinking.

This happens the other way around, too. If you find yourself judging and being frustrated by another person's behavior, ask yourself if this is triggering something that you're hard on yourself about.

When I was learning this in my life, I experimented with this idea on my children.

I found myself getting uptight during our morning routine. Stress abounded trying to get us all ready and out the door for work and school. My anger would flare when I interpreted my kids as "not helping me" in the morning. Seriously, those kids would walk out the door to the bus and never think about their backpacks unless I reminded them to grab them! Sometimes I would go bananas and yell through my frustration.

Horrified that this conflict was causing rifts in my relationship with my Leo and Lily, I decided to do something about it. Reflecting on my life, I recalled shame-filled memories of when I wasn't helpful to those around me. I also remembered a few examples of being selfish in the past when I allowed someone else to cover my slack. I understood that I was human and made mistakes and though I couldn't change the past, I could commit to being different in the future. I decided to forgive myself. I committed to being more helpful in my future even if it takes extra effort. This relieved emotions that I didn't even know I had, but were feeding my impatience with my kids in the morning.

After a few weeks of practicing this awareness and forgiveness for old transgressions each time I got angry, the mornings became more peaceful around our house. When I was more patient with myself, I was more patient with them. With the awareness and agency, I was also able to ask for what I wanted them to do instead of getting frustrated and complaining.[22] That small practice changed our mornings and our relationships.

---

22   Watch the video on this: jodiaman.com/make-or-break-your-relationships/

People often think they're supposed to get over their problems alone and are so ashamed for even *wishing* they could reach out that they don't dare actually reach out. But no one does things alone. If you are hard on yourself for being too needy, keep in mind that even great leaders have teams of helpers. Humans are social beings who depend on families, partners and communities for biological, mental and emotional sustenance. Evolution created us this way to maximize survival. Because of this, your heart and soul long to feel connected. Don't let your insecurity keep you from getting close to people.

Anxiety wants us isolated. Countering this is one of the most important pieces of your recovery. Reaching out and connecting with others will help you in many ways.

- Conversations take you out of your head and into the present.
- Other's ideas, jokes and stories can be distracting.
- Helping other people makes you feel good about yourself.
- A friend's company encourages you through challenging activities.
- You will be relieved to know you're not the only one to feel this way.
- Nothing heals or feels better than the power of love. You'll also find that connecting with animals helps to ease your anxiety. Fear and worries are washed away by connecting, loving, petting and breathing with animals. Countless people when they feel anxious go to their loving pets and receive the instant relief of unconditional love. Animals make you feel warm and decrease your stress hormones, lowering your heart rate.[23] Because animals are always in the present moment, they provide a good model for you to be mindful.

---

23   J.K. Vormbrock and J.M. Grossberg, "Cardiovascular effects of human-pet dog interactions," *Journal of Behavioral Medicine* 11, no. 5 (October 1988): 509-17.

Your loved ones long to be loved and needed, just like you do. They will feel relieved there is someone out there who feels just like them, too. You contribute to their life and purpose. There are people you feel happy around and other people who bring you down. Take control of who you spend your time with. Make conscious decisions that will have you around the happy people, and soon you will be a happy person whom others want to be around.

Connecting is essential to getting over anxiety. Without close relationships, it's easy to feel alone and unloved. This is most unsettling. Getting connected is the quickest way to heal.

Take action

Pick one or more people who know and care about you from your past or present. You can connect with them by thinking of how they influenced you, even if they're not with you physically. Write the name(s) here.

_____

_____

_____

Think about them and ask yourself:
What does he/she appreciate about me?

_____

_____

_____

How did he/she contribute to how I am today?

_____

_____

_____

_____

What did I contribute to his/her life?

_____

_____

_____

Skill #7: Find a Higher Priority

"I can't stay here."

Overwhelmed with anxiety, I looked into my husband's eyes, searching for understanding and strength. We were on a blanket with our two boys on the lawn outside the town hall, waiting for the Fourth of July fireworks to begin. Panic was bubbling in my chest. It was hard to sit still. Attempting some kind of control, I decided leaving might prevent my rising anxiety from getting worse.

Ted understood and let me take our younger son, who was a toddler, to my car. *Thank God we drove separately*, I thought.

I couldn't get out of there fast enough, eager to reach the safety of my house. This was crazy, because I panicked at home just as much as anywhere else, but I was desperately trying to outrun anxiety.

Relief washed over me as I arrived at the car, buckled Leo into his car seat and pulled out of my parking space. *I made it!*

Fireworks were one of my favorite things when I was young, but at this point I didn't care. I just wanted to get home. That was my priority.

Then, I turned onto the main street and got totally stuck in fireworks traffic. My car had nowhere to move. I was at a dead stop. *Oh my God! Oh my God!*

Sitting there, trying not to freak out, I saw the first firework go off. It was beautiful. Leo squirmed and protested being locked in his car seat. *Breathe, Jodi.*

Leo started crying. Anxiety had to take a backseat as my maternal instincts took over. I couldn't leave my son upset and not comfort him. I pulled over to the curb and within a minute Leo was bouncing on my lap, watching the display out of the windshield. He flapped his arms and laughed at the lights exploding above us. Anxiety almost made me miss this — witnessing Leo's wonder and joy, which gave *me* wonder and joy. It was then I realized how many things anxiety had caused me to miss. I avoided so many events and opportunities, because I didn't think I could handle having anxiety at them. The worst part is that I did things separately from the rest of my family. That wasn't okay with me. I was giving anxiety too much power over my decisions and I had to stop. Experiencing joy with my family was too important to me.

Panic can have you missing life's beauty. Too often you say to yourself, "I don't want to do it anyway." But it's not a true, "don't want to."

When you picture yourself going somewhere, you see yourself uncomfortable there. That doesn't sound pleasant and you think you don't want to go. It doesn't seem worth the trouble. You think of it as pointless. When this happens, you need to find a point to what you are doing. Something that is important enough to push through the anxiety, something to take priority over "remaining comfortable" so that you do what you've been afraid of doing. Anxiety doesn't like this. It wants you to think that nothing is worth it, because "it will be too awful" (Tricks 1, 3, 6, 13, and 15).

Missy

Missy was ten-years-old. She had a fear of fire equipment after her grandfather died in a fire. When she visited her mom's office, she was afraid of going down the hallway, because she would see the exit signs and sprinklers.

On one visit, not long after we started meeting, she wanted cookies from the vending machine and decided that this was more important than worrying about her fears. She walked down the hallway to get the snack. If she didn't want the treat badly enough, she would have said, "That's okay, I don't really want cookies." But she *did* want them. In that moment, they were more important than staying comfortable. She did it — and realized that she *could* do it — and the next time she walked down the hall, it was easier.

Sheree

Sheree was afraid of driving on the expressway. We decided to practice together as part of therapy. But she delayed this over and over, preferring to sit and talk about more pressing problems rather than deal with that one. The thing was, she managed getting around. Even though it was a bit inconvenient driving on side streets, she could reach anywhere she needed to go. There was no urgency to getting rid of this fear.

When she brought it up again, I asked her, "If one of your children was in the hospital and you were trying to get to him, would you drive on the expressway if it was the fastest way?"

She exclaimed a full-hearted, "Yes!"

Getting to her child would be a clear priority over preventing her anxiety.

Sometimes, like for me, the desire to get your life back from anxiety is enough of a priority. Let this be yours, too. Because getting your life back means having adventure, relationships, confidence, peace of mind and laughter. All worth every ounce of effort.

Even though happiness, fun and connecting to loved ones are important to you, the desperation to avoid possible anxiety-provoking situations may still be winning out. That's why having tangible, or multiple, priorities help.

Priorities change depending on the context. Children are a priority in the life of parents, but when they're happy, safe and occupied, taking a phone call might be more important than sitting with them. Other times a mom may be at a business meeting, but an emergency call from her child's school will have her excusing herself. Priorities depend on what is going on in the moment. If you're struggling with anxiety, find both immediate priorities and life priorities so you are covered.

Anxiety wants you to think that you can't do things and acts as if that limit is definite. Don't be resigned to anxiety's limits on your life. They're not true limits. Doing it is possible. You can do it, it just seems hard, vulnerable and uncomfortable, but it's usually not as bad as anxiety has you imagining.

It's about finding motivation. A lot of times it's easier to do something for someone else than to do something for yourself. Old-fashioned, self-help advice would say, "You should do this for yourself."

I'd say, "Who cares? Whatever gets you going is great!" It's noble to be motivated by your love. Never judge yourself for that. Anything you treasure can motivate — a band, a project, food, a relationship, money, an experience, helping someone, luxury, fun and on and on.

When you're in physical danger, you do things you'd never imagine having the courage to do. You do them, because you're highly motivated to survive physically, mentally and spiritually.

The choice is simple — do them or don't survive. The action helps control the fear.

If you're not in physical danger, find something that motivates you. Something precious that means the world to you — that has you taking action despite your fears. The action will overpower the anxiety. Repeating it will make you more and more comfortable, and soon the anxiety will go away.

Take action

Make a list of people, things or issues that are important to you.

_____

_____

_____

_____

_____

Looking at your list, circle who/what inspires and motivates you to face your fears?

How can you use this to push through your fears?

_____

_____

_____

_____

_____

Skill #8: Practice Exposure

Inaction breeds doubt and fear. Action breeds confidence and courage. If you want to conquer fear, do not sit home and think about it. Go out and get busy.

~Dale Carnegie

Jill

Jill came to me with a paralyzing anxiety about throwing up. The fear had been limiting her life for the last decade or so. Her family couldn't talk about nausea in front of her. A vomiting scene in a movie would ruin her *week*. She was even afraid to get into a serious relationship, because she was embarrassed to tell her lover that she had emetophobia. Jill felt that her life was out of control. She was desperate to regain some control and find relief, but said she had no hope that she could change this problem.

The first thing we did was build her confidence and her sense of personal agency. Through initial therapeutic conversations, we discovered a wise, inner voice that spoke to her during panic attacks. It said things like, "This is a panic attack. I have never thrown up during a panic attack. Just breathe. It will pass."

This inner reassurance calmed her down in a matter of ten to twenty minutes. *Ten to twenty minutes!* That seemed fast and amazing to me. My panic attacks used to last four or five hours!

I asked Jill if she thought getting rid of anxiety in ten to twenty minutes using her wise voice seemed like "control" to her. The surprise showed on her face. This was a new way to see it. It was the first time she experienced herself as having power. In our conversation, she explained that the last time she threw up eleven years ago, she remembered feeling "relief immediately after" purging. Anxiety had her forgetting that part. (Trick # 7.)

By some strange cosmic coincidence, between our first and second sessions, Jill and her whole family became ill with a stomach bug. (I know. Can you believe it? What are the chances?) Jill was the only one in the house who made it through the virus without vomiting. *Talk about control!*

She told me that she was amazed by this ability.

"And I wasn't even that nervous!" she added.

By our third session, Jill felt it was possible to get over her fear, saying: "I feel like I will be able to."

She was building confidence and feeling empowered after suffering her powerlessness for so long. She wanted to stimulate a nauseous sensation, because she felt ready for the challenge of it. What a change in *three* sessions! She was no longer afraid of being afraid and that made all the difference.

I suggested we watch people throw up on YouTube as a first step of graduated exposure therapy.[24] Wanting to be free from her phobia took priority over being comfortable, and she agreed.

With the sound off, we watched a video of men on a roller coaster to ease her in. This had a surprising effect on us. We began to laugh! The videos of people throwing up were hysterical. Laughter and anxiety can't live in the same moment together. Laughing felt too good!

We watched another video, which was a bit more graphic, and she still laughed. Then, we graduated to one with sound. The two of us were rolling on the floor clutching our sides. Ten years of panic went right out the window. She planned to go home and keep watching. She never came back to therapy. I checked in with her by email and she said her panic was gone.

---

24   Jonathan S. Abramowitz, Brett Jason Deacon, and Stephen P.H. Whiteside, *Exposure Therapy for Anxiety: Principles and Practice* (New York: Guilford Press, 2010).

Exposure therapy was introduced to the Western world by James G. Taylor[25] (1897–1973) from South Africa in the 1950s. It has been used as a method of helping people face their fears. First, patients are taught skills in calming themselves. Then, they go through a process of slowly exposing themselves to what they are afraid of so that it becomes familiar and less intimidating.

This may sound scary. *Do it? That's the whole problem. I can't do it!*

The idea that you "can't" is a perception only, not a truth. Avoiding something because you're afraid is just *thinking* you can't. It doesn't *mean* that you can't.

Here's a summary of the above steps, in case you want to try it.

1. Commit to making an effort to heal.
2. Break down the power of anxiety first by calling it out on its lies.
3. Take action: Go beyond your comfort zone, starting small and building confidence, gradually working your way up to bigger challenges.
4. Love yourself through it. Have total compassion — without negative self-judgment — and celebrate every step of the way.

If you wait until you have no fear before doing something, you may never do it.

Take action

Start with steps 1–3. Commit to making an effort to heal by writing down what you want to do, if fear didn't stop you.

1. Disempower anxiety by listing why your fears are unnecessary.

---

25   Joseph Wolpe and David Wolpe, *Our Useless Fears* (Boston: Houghton Mifflin Company, 1981).

2. Decide on the first small step.

Here are some examples of commitments:

Today, I will exercise without letting fear stop me.

Today, I will speak up to my co-worker without letting fear stop me.

This week, I will tell Josie how I feel.

This month, I will clean out the closet without letting fear stop me.

1. Complete these sentences.

Today, I will

_____

without letting fear stop me.

This week, I will

_____

without letting fear stop me.

This month, I will

_____

without letting fear stop me.

This year, I will

_____

without letting fear stop me.

2. This is why my fears are unnecessary…

_____

_____

_____

_____

_____

_____

_____

3. This is the first small step to doing what I want.

_____

_____

_____

_____

_____

_____

Skill #9: "Harry Potter" It

So the boggart sitting in the darkness within has not yet assumed a form. He does not yet know what will frighten the person on the other side of the door. Nobody knows what a boggart looks like when he is alone, but when I let him out, he will immediately become whatever each of us most fears.

~J.K. Rowling, as Professor Lupine

This is my favorite skill! J.K. Rowling really tackled fear and anxiety in her *Harry Potter* stories in brilliant ways. Having courage in the face of adversity was one of the main themes in this series. For example, in *Harry Potter and the Prisoner of Azkaban*, Rowling introduced the dark mythical creature called "boggart" — a name she borrowed from a malevolent spirit in English folklore. In Harry Potter's fictional world, a boggart is a nasty bugger found hiding in cupboards or other small containers. Whoever is present when it's let loose suffers greatly, because when it comes out of hiding, the boggart shape-shifts into the object of one's worst fear.

It's horrific! (Thankfully it's fictional — or is it?) It sounds a lot like anxiety, doesn't it? The person's mind controls what the boggart becomes.

What makes it more interesting and pertinent is the incantation — the magical spell to get rid of the boggart — which is to say *"Riddikulus!"* while changing the fear into something humorous.

The students take turns practicing as the boggart changes from a mummy, to a severed hand, to a spider. Each student yelling, *"Riddukulus!"* and changing the object of their fear into something funny. The boggart gets confused. The class is in stitches and they're able to pop the boggart out of existence.

Fear usually confuses us, but what if we confused it back?

Anxiety often runs in your head as a scene of something horrible happening. You need to change that into something less scary and less disturbing, just like the students do with the boggart, so that you stop stimulating the sympathetic nervous system and your body calms down. If you replace the terrifying scene with a vision full of hope or something funny, you will have a greater sense of control and dismiss your fears.

The imagined scenes are powerful, because they're scary and have us running away. What if instead you went toward your fear? Harry and Professor Lupine seek out boggarts, so Harry can practice going against what frightens him. Practicing is the key here.

Every time you feel anxious, it's an opportunity to practice your skills, like Cara looking forward to the babysitter coming from Trick #8. If you practice them on purpose rather than when you're blindsided by anxiety, it puts you in a better position when anxiety does come. When you work out, you become stronger. When you practice a sport, you improve. When you cook a lot, you start to know what works when preparing different types of foods and which spices to add to get the best results. Practice isn't hard, but so often overlooked.

Practice makes you agile. And you're able to anticipate what's coming from a more informed position, because you've been there before in less stressful circumstances. But, with anxiety you mistakenly think you either can do something or you can't (Trick #2: Black and White Thinking). But if you can't do it now, you can practice and be able to later. We know this, but anxiety is invested in having us forget what we know. The more you practice, the more confidence you build. It's trust in yourself that makes all the difference.

The power of this confidence is illustrated in the end of the movie. Harry lives through a devastating night and then goes back in time to change what happens. The first time through the scenario, something saves Harry and his godfather from a fate worse than death. When he goes back in time, he watches himself go through everything again, waiting to find out who saves him. When no one comes, he realizes that it is he who saves them and is able to conjure an advanced and powerful charm despite his novice abilities. He tells his friend Hermione:

"I knew I could do it...Because I'd already done it"

Harry succeeds, because he trusted himself knowing he was already successful in the past. When anxiety comes and tells us we can't do something, we've forgotten that a lot of the time we've already done it. We made it through once before and can do it again.

Rowling gives many helpful strategies: You have the power to change the object of your fear into something less intimidating, silly or even funny. You can practice a skill to improve it and this builds your confidence. You can remember a past time when you did something similar and had success. All of these will help you overcome your fear and take action toward what you want in your life.

Take action

If you personified your fear, what would it look like? Draw it below.

Make it silly. Write a funny poem about it. Draw it in a ridiculous way. Tell a goofy story to take the power right out of it.

Skill #10: Nourish Yourself

I'm vulnerable to anxiety when I don't get enough rest. Sleep deprivation has thrown me off-kilter too many times not to make getting eight hours a priority in my life. That's just one way I nourish myself physically, emotionally, mentally and spiritually that helped me get past my anxiety.

When you take care of yourself, you're less susceptible to emotional problems. Loads of people are suffering so much in their anxiety, and yet they totally neglect basic, self-care activities that could change their life. It's time to change that. It's not hard, but takes discipline. (It's surely not as difficult as suffering through anxiety!) Here are seven important ways you can nourish yourself.

1. Sleep enough.
2. Eat whole foods.
3. Stay warm.
4. Practice compassion.
5. Exercise.

6. Meditate.

7. Be creative.

These ideas won't be new to you. If they're not part of your day, think about what's keeping you from nourishing yourself. For me, it was procrastination. I could always do it tomorrow. If you feel like you're working vigorously to feel better, but you've left out some or most of the things on this list, this may be why you don't see progress. Let's get you reprioritized.

Sleep enough.

Sleep is one of the most important ways to take care of your health, but it's the first thing to go if you're too busy. Also, when your body is loaded with cortisol, it is hyper-alert and energized, making it hard to sleep. Sleeping improves mood, skin, immunity, learning skills, physical health, memory, weight maintenance, sex drive, judgment and agility.

When improving your sleep habits, the first action to focus on is routine. Go to bed at the same time each night and wake up at the same time each morning. Have a bedtime routine that includes some relaxing activities, like a bath, self-massage and meditation.

(Get my sleep hygiene handout on the book resource page: jodiaman.com/you1anxiety0.)

Eat whole foods.

Eating right makes you feel better. This is hard to do when your eating is controlled by your emotions.[26] Sometimes you eat bad food as a comfort, or you restrict yourself as a punishment. The way to change this unhealthy way of eating is to change your relationship with food.

---

26 This is a huge topic which can fill a library of books. I will only mention a few ideas here to point you in the right direction, but if this is something that is an issue for you, kindly make addressing it a priority.

Your emotions and the way you feel about the food you're eating gets digested into you right along with any meal. Try to eat when you're happy rather than guilty or ashamed. At the very least you can be grateful about the food. Think about food as nourishment and say "Yes!" to everything you put in your mouth. A great way to do this is to keep a food journal, or take a picture of everything you eat. This activity forces you to be aware of what you're eating, which alone helps you make healthier decisions.

Eating whole foods is a good rule of thumb. Whole foods are as close to their original forms as you can get. If you're ready to tackle eating better, change one thing at a time. Keep in mind that caffeine, sugar, carbonated beverages, alcohol and artificial sweeteners are terrible for anxiety. Eat soups and stews or drink hot liquid, especially in the winter[27] when anxiety is higher.

Stay warm.

Ayurveda, the traditional Hindu system of medicine based on balance in bodily systems that uses diet, herbal treatment and yogic breathing, teaches you to get warm to calm your anxiety. Take a shower or bath, or drink hot milk, soup, or tea. In the winter, it's important to move your body to create warmth from within to feel empowered rather than trapped by the cold weather. You can get to know your body type and read about ways to pacify your intense emotions from the vast literature on Ayurveda.[28]

Practice self-compassion.

I can't stress enough how important it is to be more kind to yourself. It's the most important thing you can do to heal yourself. I can argue

---

27   Anxiety is higher in the winter because of the cold, the dryness, the long nights, feeling trapped inside, and lack of distractions.
28   Vasant Lad, Ayurveda: *The Science of Self-Healing: A Practical Guide* (Twin Lakes, Wisconsin: Lotus Press, 1985).

that it's the *only* thing you have to do, because once you do that, everything else takes care of itself. For this reason, I've dedicated the sixth chapter solely to this.

Exercise.

Moving your body builds your confidence. The best way to raise your self-esteem is to commit to a daily activity and follow through with it. Exercise is great for this. You get the added physiological benefits of tryptophan and endorphins, feel-good hormones, a fit body and a time to release stress and clear your mind. The relaxing hormone, tryptophan is only a small molecule.[29] Larger molecules go into your brain every day and tryptophan has trouble competing. However, when you exercise, the larger molecules move down to your muscles and the tryptophan goes straight up to your head, helping you feel calmer, happy and you sleep better, too.

Exercise is a win-win-win-win. Don't leave it out of your day.

Meditate.

Taking a few minutes a day to quiet your mind can change your life. I use it in my own life and with my clients all of the time. There are many studies on the benefits of meditation touting that it improves your immunity, skin and overall health, reduces pain, anxiety and blood pressure, and raises your mood, confidence and energy.

I can attest that meditation has made physical, emotional and spiritual improvements in my life. I put together a 21-day meditation program called *Living Free*. You can get that series here: 21guidedmeditations.com.

Be creative.

Your vivid imagination is used against you by anxiety when you

---

29   Tae Woon Ki et al., "Stress-Induced Depression Is Alleviated by Aerobic Exercise Through Up-Regulation of 5-Hydroxytryptamine 1A Receptors in Rats," *International Neurourology Journal* 19, no. 1 (March 2015): 27–33

picture worst-case scenarios. Anxiety needs brain space to spin its tales of terror. The best way to counter this is to use your brain space for more creative projects.

Humans are made to create. When you're not in any kind of creative process, your soul begins to wither. Your unoccupied brain has time to delve into negative emotions like anxiety and guilt, and you can get immobilized. The fastest way to jump-start any healing is to be creative.[30] This could mean crafts, but it can be so much more than that. Creating is any kind of problem-solving endeavor. You create a resolution. You use your brain to figure out how you're going to do something. Your brain is making decisions to create the best possible result.

Here are some examples. Organize an event, find something you're looking for, clean out a closet, remake furniture, plan how to decrease your spending, fix something, write, cook... The list is endless.

Creating distracts you, builds confidence and hones problem-solving skills.

Nourishing yourself is a worthy and empowering thing you can do to help yourself when any problem arises. It has immediate and lasting benefits. Once these skills become a habit, they're easy and enjoyable ways to take care of yourself.

Take action

Go to my Pinterest page: pinterest.com/jodiaman and check out my Nourish Yourself community board.

Commit to one daily nourishing practice right now.

---

30   Clara Parkes, *The Yarn Whisperer: Reflections of a Life in Knitting* (New York: Abrams, 2013).

I am going to add this to my morning routine…

Skill #11: Believe You Can

Leslie

Leslie (from Trick #2) had endured unspeakable emotional and physical trauma from personal violence and war over a long period of time. She and I were talking about her anxiety.

"The littlest things are upsetting me," Leslie said.

"Can you give me an example?"

"Okay. Like, I was driving on the thruway and decided I would use the nearest rest stop to go to the ladies' room. But when I came upon the very next one, I unintentionally drove past it. I started to panic and got so mad at myself for missing it. I couldn't breathe and had to pull over to settle myself down. I kept thinking, *This is so stupid to be upset about! What is wrong with me? I can just go to the next one.*"

So many things can trigger an old memory to rise up and take over your emotions. It's even worse when those memories are from a traumatic event. A smell, a shape, a sound, a touch, a person — anything your senses take in can send you emotionally back to a threatening incident from your past. It might be in the form of a nightmare, a flashback or an anxiety attack. The suffering from this is intense.

It can also be incredibly frustrating and disappointing that even though you're presently safe, you feel the panic as though you're still in danger. You beat yourself up, because your reaction seems crazy and over-the-top for that trigger. For Leslie, she was distracted and overwhelmed by the power of her panic when she could have simply gone to the next rest stop and be fine. This negative self-judgment is like pouring a gasoline on glowing embers.

Leslie actually had two reactions. Her initial reaction, the fear response, is understandable given her history. "Mistakes" are an emotional memory that triggers her amygdala to release hormones. However, she didn't see it that way. She saw this first reaction as a mistake too, which increased the intensity of her feelings and caused her second reaction, self-loathing.

The first reaction was biology; the second is undeserved and increased the length and degree of her suffering. Most people don't realize they're having two reactions because the negative self-judgment and intensification happens so immediately. Like Leslie, all they can see is they're crazy enough to let a little thing upset them.

I helped Leslie understand her emotional response and uncover why she felt upset.

"When you were in a situation of danger — like during abuse, shootings and bombings — you needed acute skills of survival. Constant care and vigilance is how you made it through. These skills meant your next breath. You needed them and, thank goodness, you had them.

"Despite being currently safe in your life, your brain will still be triggered into the panic by even little disappointments, changes and mistakes because in the past these meant danger. You were blamed and attacked for the slightest misstep. Even small errors (and no errors) instigated violence. You're not weird or crazy because your sympathetic system was triggered when you missed the rest stop. It's understandable."

Once Leslie understands why she responds with panic, then she doesn't have to freak out on herself any more. Instead, it would be lovely to say to herself, "I understand why I'd feel upset, but it's okay now. I am safe. Thanks, Body, for being ready if I needed you. You've helped me so much! Thank you! I wouldn't be alive if it weren't for you and this immediate response. Everything is okay right now. You can relax." And then she'd need to keep gently speaking to herself for the few minutes while her body calms down. This will help her feel empowered and good about herself, instead of like she's *crazypants*. Rather than feeling like her panic comes out of the blue for no reason, she will honor her skills and believe in herself. If every time Leslie is triggered, she does this, then after a while her brain will get rid of that trigger.

If you've made it this far, you have survived hardship. You can say, "It's no big deal. I didn't have it as bad as other people." But that's undermining yourself and your experience. Stop thinking your efforts mean nothing. Bottom line is that you survived. You handled situations that came to you. Everything you did, you did with a purpose to survive, protect yourself, help someone else, prevent something and more. Acting with purpose means something was or is important to you.

See how amazing you are for all of that. Celebrate your awesomeness (even the littlest steps) and begin to believe in yourself. When you believe in yourself, anxiety doesn't have power. Trust yourself and live your life in relative peace. Take risks, have adventures, get close to people and find joy in challenges, and feel so alive while doing it!

Take action

Celebrate YOU. Make a poster displaying a list of your skills, knowledges and accomplishments. If you have trouble, ask a loved one for help. Refer back to this list often. Decorate it, make it your own, and post it somewhere prominent. Take a photo of it with your phone, so you can look at it anytime.

Skill #12: Lighten Up

Tammy, Betsy, and Tim

Tammy worries intensely that something is going to go wrong and thinks she needs to be constantly vigilant so she doesn't miss a possible mistake and fail to fix it. Betsy has difficulty taking a compliment like, "You are so kind." When she hears it, she immediately detracts it. "Everyone does it. People are supposed to do that," she says — not humbly, but in a degrading way. However, if something were to go wrong — even if it has nothing to do with her — she immediately figures out how she is to blame.

Tim thinks that he has to keep working hard to heal. When he feels sad or panicked, he hunkers down and says, "Okay, I have to figure this out." He thinks himself into a flurry of self-doubt and panic and feels like he's losing his mind. His cortisol levels increase, which makes him try to work harder, which makes him feel more like a failure — and he spirals out of control.

The three of them are taking themselves very seriously. When they do this, the meaning of everything increases a hundredfold. If something is bad, it feels devastating. If some error occurs, it feels life-threatening. If someone has doubt, he feels utterly lost. Every little thing seems personal. They feel vulnerable and "messed up." Life itself appears to be overwhelming. This is fraught with negative self-judgment and an absence of joy.

Feeling bad doesn't mean that there's something wrong with you. It just means that your thinking has gotten a bit out of control. It happens easily and to many people. You may be thinking that it's only you, because everyone else gets over things fast. The fact is, they just hide it well. Our culture creates and sustains anxiety and then we label it as wrong. Feeling shame, we all hide it. We suffer in silence and feel more alone. Then, it feels more "serious."

What would happen if you didn't take yourself so seriously? What if you laughed at your more ridiculous worries? You know the ones I mean, like worrying that you'll fall down the drain or that a ghost car will snatch you from the bus stop. If you laughed at these instead of freaking out and judging them, you'd feel totally different. Instead of being beaten down and exhausted, you'd feel light and relieved. Remember, laughter stops anxiety. Watch funny movies. Read funny books. Spend time with funny people. Stop being so hard on yourself and stop calling yourself stupid. *You are not stupid!*

Personifying anxiety and worry helps me separate it from my sense of myself. Helping kids think about worry this way is empowering. Saying, "Go away, Worry!" has them think of the worry differently. It works partly because it's silly and fun, but mostly because it reminds them that their worry is not part of who they are and can disappear.

Mike

The easiest way to lighten up is to have compassion for yourself. This is exactly what I told eighteen-year-old Mike. A few weeks before we met, his girlfriend lost her battle with cancer. His deep grief was a testimony to how much he loved her and how connected the two of them had been. But in addition to his devastating loss, Mike was stuck in a prison of conflicting negative self-judgments. In his mind, he was not allowed to be sad that his girlfriend died because, "It would make her feel guilty." And, "It's weak." Then, he wasn't allowed to *not* be sad, because that would suggest that he "didn't care enough about her."

The poor boy, who was such a loving, caring person, had nowhere left to stand. This put him in a constant state of panic, so intense that he rarely left his room except to meet with me. I asked if he could lighten up by having more compassion for himself.

Through tears, he asked, "How?"

I started to cry, too. Humans are rarely taught how to do this.

I told him, "It's like you're not allowed to feel any way. Not happy. Not sad.

"But your feelings are exactly what anyone would feel in your shoes. It'd be weird if you didn't feel them. They mean you are a good, loving, caring person. They mean Becca was special to you. It's okay to feel them.

So, whatever you feel, just say to yourself, *'This is okay. I am okay to feel this way.'* And mean it. That's compassion. Just say, *'I get it.'* to yourself.

"Then, instead of overthinking the situation and burying yourself in overwhelming emotions trying to figure it out, you'll be able to stop thinking and move on to some other activity that's benign and pleasant."

It's not the feeling that causes suffering, it's the story and meaning around it. Taking things seriously wreaks more havoc. All those worries and negative self-judgments aren't true or deserved. Lighten up about your mistakes and worries, be more understanding and compassionate with yourself, and you'll feel the weight on your shoulders lightening, too.

Take action

Write out some feelings you have about something that happened recently. Beside each feeling write "…and I understand why I feel that way," or "… and it's okay that I feel that way." See my examples. Read what you write aloud to yourself.

1. "I'm hurt when nobody helps me….and I understand why I feel that way."
2. "I was angry that she blew me off…and it's okay to feel that way."

3. _____

_____

_____

4. _____

_____

_____

5. _____

_____

_____

6. _____

_____

_____

Skill #13: Talk About It

Anxiety is often instigated by two things, feelings in your body, and thoughts in your head. It may be hard for you to distinguish which comes first. One brings on the other almost without us noticing. But once you consciously realize you're anxious, it's the mind that keeps it going.[31] Therefore, it's the mind that you have to

---

31   Unless it is a medical issue that sustains the sympathetic nervous system response, for example high cortisol levels from chronic stress, hyperthyroidism, low vitamin D or Bs, etc

contend with. One surefire way to take anxiety down a notch is to say your fear out loud. Express in words what you're afraid of, either to a friend or an empty room.

Doing this gets the anxiety out of your head and invites you (or the friend) to be an audience to it. This gives you distance from the chaos, so you can see it from a new perspective. You can reason with it. What holds power inside your mind sounds ridiculous when spoken aloud. This gives you a leg up, and you have the power to make a choice about whether or not you're going to stay afraid. You have energy and wherewithal and can *do* something. Not only has anxiety's control over you diminished, but you have the stamina to counter the rest of it.

Sometimes people assume that if you say your worries out loud, you'll be overwhelmed by intense negative emotion (Paul from Trick #14). You fear that if you don't hold it all together, you'll risk falling off that insanity cliff. Making you feel vulnerable to that is just anxiety's tactic to keep you powerless. There is no insanity cliff to fall off.

Shame often makes us keep fears to ourselves. You're ashamed of feeling anxious in the first place or you're anxious about something you are ashamed of. None of the shame is warranted, because your fears are probably strikingly similar to everyone else's. You're not weird or different. You are human.

Shame can do a number on you, keeping you stuck and silent in a place where you feel unworthy, unloved and doomed. Silence becomes a rule to hold you together, but it only makes things worse.

Kelly

Recently, I spoke with Kelly, who is four years old, about her worries. Her mom told me that these began just a month before, when she refused to go to school, had tantrums about going to the store and even protested going to her grandmother's house where she spent three days a week while her mom worked. Her mother couldn't understand it.

For Kelly, the new problem of worrying and the subsequent desperation to resist leaving her house became such a focus of attention, it overshadowed the source of the problem. When her parents asked her why she refused to go somewhere, she said, "I don't want to go there."

"Why not?" they asked.

"I just don't."

They brought Kelly to see me. Since many children who grow up in unsafe or chaotic environments get worries, I first checked if something had happened to Kelly to trigger this reaction. Nothing I heard gave me the impression that she was in physical danger. Worries can come to safe little girls too — sometimes in the most random ways. Kelly's worries didn't like to be talked about (Trick #14), so it took a bit of investigation to figure out why she was so anxious. After twenty minutes, we discovered what had happened.

She had to go poo in school.

She had to go poo in school and she didn't know if this was allowed. How could she know? She never saw anybody else do it. They were all behind closed doors. Not knowing upset her tremendously, but since it was such a private matter, she was too ashamed to ask anyone. The worries and shame built up in her head, making it increasingly harder to talk about. Paralyzed, she abruptly refused to go to school, gymnastics, the grocery store or grandma's house. She was worried that she might have to go poo away from home, because "this might not be okay." During the weeks of not telling anyone about her fears, Kelly became more and more withdrawn.

When she finally told us, we could address it. We told her that she didn't need to listen to the "Poo Worry" because it was okay to poo in any restroom, in school or at the store, and even at grandma's. All bathrooms were for people to pee or poo in. Once Kelly found out that everyone pooed in bathrooms everywhere, she stopped worrying about it.

If your friends or loved ones have worries, help them talk these out. They'll have questions you can answer that could settle their minds. If you have worries, anxieties, fears and the like, talk them out. Personifying anxieties helps you talk about it. It gives fears their own identity outside of your identity (The Poo Worry). Shame is alleviated when you are no longer the problem. Without the heavy, exhausting self-blame of being crazy, there is less emotional turmoil and more empowerment to change your circumstances.

Speaking your worries aloud is a fantastic skill to have. It gets the nervous energy out. You feel less alone. You feel sane. When you voice your worries, this gives you something to push against instead of fighting yourself. Talking your fears out gives you distance and a new perspective. It helps you listen to reassurance from loved ones with new ears and calms your anxious heart.

Take action

1. Say your worries aloud to an empty room. Listen to yourself. Do they sound as bad as they do in your head? Repeat them over and over until your nervous energy decreases. You can even repeat, "I'm so scared. I'm so scared. I'm so scared. I'm so scared..." Imagine you are letting air out of a big balloon until it's very small and weak.

2. Find a friend you can text out your fears to when they come up. This should be someone you trust and who you feel doesn't judge you. Anytime you feel a worry or fear, type it out and send it to them. Allow them to dissuade your fears and help you laugh them off.

Skill #14: Ask Anxiety to Come

We gain strength, and courage, and confidence by each experience in which we really stop to look fear in the face... We must do that which we think we cannot.

~Eleanor Roosevelt

Almost two decades ago, my own personal therapist suggested "Planned Worry Time" to me. She proposed that I spend ten minutes giving myself permission to let the worries flow as intense and big as they wanted. Then at the end of ten minutes, I would halt that process and move on with my day.

To be honest, I thought she belonged in the loony bin. My anxiety was so undesirable, I couldn't fathom *letting* it come. I was too busy running away from it, fearing it would consume me, and being desperate for my life back. Giving it permission was a new paradigm, and I couldn't get my head around it. I firmly rejected this technique.

Over the years, as a therapist myself, I've had many clients refuse skills and ideas that I witnessed helping many others. *That's stupid. It won't work for me. I don't believe in that.*

I know anxiety doesn't want them to get better and it will work hard to keep them oppressed under its rule, including coming up with excuses not to try something that would make them feel better. Just like I did when it was my turn. When we are so overwhelmed by the chaos of anxiety, holding on for dear life, risks are unwelcome. First, we need to build up our courage and faith in ourselves, before we feel safe enough to open our mind to a new idea.

It wasn't until much later, once I'd built up my confidence in myself, that Planned Worry Time seemed feasible and I tried it. As a young girl, I was terrorized by images in my head of demons, ghouls, decomposing flesh and other evil creatures. I tried to push these out of my mind, but this made them more threatening. Once I trusted myself more, I realized my fear was feeding the images' power (Trick #8: Anxiety Scares You) and I decided to deliberately "stare" at them (in my imagination) instead of running away.

Since it was my conscious choice, I felt in control. I held the images in my mind and an unexpected thing happened. They faded. I tried to get them back clearer and they faded again! I stayed in the present moment with my goal to keep the images front and center in my mind. That action took my focus instead of fear and anxiety. The ghouls kept fading away despite my efforts to keep them there, and I never got anxious.

After practicing this for a couple of weeks, when I was feeling okay, I built confidence enough to use the technique when I was already anxious. Over time this practice retrained my amygdala to stop being triggered by these pictures in my mind. I've never had anxiety again with those scary images to this day.

A few years ago, I began to notice that I would get freaky images in my mind about my bloody fingers. I would see my hands in a blender, being cut by gardening shears or in the garbage disposal. This happened more and more frequently and was very disturbing.

Why is my mind doing this? I worried.

People commonly have random thoughts like crashing their car, seeing themselves dead, cutting themselves and the like. This doesn't seem normal and makes them feel crazy and ashamed. So much so, that the thoughts intensify and come more often.

There are thousands of thoughts going through your mind every day. Some come and go quickly, barely registering. But the mind especially grabs thoughts that are either familiar or weird.

For example, if you generally feel inadequate in life and have a thought about someone being mad at you, your mind will give it attention. You begin to analyze it, allowing it to take on its own energy and spin out of control. Soon, all the past examples of people not liking you and you messing up relationships come into your mind, building ever more evidence that you're inadequate. Your mind can become consumed by the thoughts, making it hard to concentrate on anything else. You become heavy with the idea of how terrible you are, and the self-berating continues from there.

Reflecting on my bloody finger episodes, I noticed that when my mind had been startled and confused, saying, "Hey, this is weird, why is it happening again?", that it was me *deciding it was weird*. This made me wonder, *Is it the thought that's disturbing or how I think about it?* I experimented. When the bloody images came to my mind, I chose to look at them and say, without any judgment at all, "Oh that's silly and random!" and refocus my energy elsewhere. I practiced allowing the images, if they came, without judgment for weeks.

This completely changed the effect they had on me. I stopped worrying about them. They didn't get out of control. And the best part was that the images came less and less frequently until finally stopping altogether. It was like me staring at the scary faces. The fear of them made them bad. Without the fear they dissolved.

That's why this is one of the last skills on our list. In the last two chapters you've learned to loosen the hold anxiety has on your life and build up confidence so it's less daunting to allow worry to come.

It helps me to remember that some people seek out the adrenaline rush. They ride fast boats, play extreme sports or jump out of airplanes to feel that energy flowing through their bodies. Others, like me, feel that same adrenaline rush in a *bad* way, because they feel like they're failing at life. They feel terrified and vulnerable. Same feeling, totally different meaning. What makes some people feel vibrantly alive and others desperate for anxiety relief? The difference is that some people think it's fun and others think it's scary. You have to think anxiety is scary for it to take over your life. Thinking that it's horrible is what gives it all the power.

Remember Cara who was afraid of having a babysitter? We used this skill. Once we built her confidence that she could calm herself, she saw the night differently. She wanted a babysitter, saying, "I hope anxiety comes tonight so I can show it who's boss." She went from terrified to pumped and ready for action.

Anxiety needs you to be scared. I've been there. Anxiety feels terrible and terrifying, so it's hard not to be scared. But you can turn the tables by asking anxiety to come. Fake bravado when speaking to *Anxiety*, and soon this practicing will help you truly feel it.

Take action

Organize a call with a good friend to catch up, have your favorite movie cued up, or set up an activity that brings you joy and comfort.

Just before you do that, try Planned Worry Time. Set a timer for a few minutes. Give yourself permission to let all your worries flow as intense and as big as they feel. Write them down, draw them, speak them, or whatever helps you get them from inside of you to the outside. Don't judge them. If they stop, keep asking more to come.

When the timer goes off, thank your worries graciously for coming out. Close the session with some empowering, encouraging words to yourself like, "I did it! I'm awesome!" Do a victory dance and head right into the activity you've set up.

Skill #15: Remember What You Know

Tally

Twenty-five-year-old Tally was overwhelmed by fears and frequent panic attacks. She was afraid that her husband would leave her or that he would die. She was afraid he'd get mad at her. She was afraid something bad would happen. It consumed her night and day. When she felt the panic coming she felt crazy and prayed for it to end soon.

Sick of it all, she came to see me for help. I already knew Tally, because she saw me a few years before when she was recovering from an eating disorder (another kind of anxiety). I remembered from our first meetings that Tally is an exceptional human being. However, when she was overwhelmed, she could not see her greatness. Anxiety clouded her view of herself. She called herself a "hopeless loser."

In our first conversation, we caught up on her life since I last saw her, and I began to write down what I heard that stood out as counter to the anxiety story she told me when setting up the appointment. When she was done filling me in on her family, her career and her social contexts, I had a substantial list of skills and abilities that I heard.

I asked her about the skills I noted from our conversation, reading them back to her in her own words. (As with many other people who think they are a "hopeless loser," she was surprised that I recorded so many.)

"You are careful with money?" I asked.

"Yes, I'm careful with money."

I look down and read the next one, "Your mom says you are emotionally mature for being twenty-five years old?"

"Yes, lot of people tell me that I'm mature for my age."

I continued questioning her about each skill and she confirmed them. I handed her some paper and she began to write a list of what we noticed. Once we had a few, it was easy to find more. We guessed what her family and husband might add. This is what we came up with. See Figure 6.

Tally knew these things (she had told me about them), but didn't *know* she knew them. Anxiety wants you to forget what you know about yourself just enough so you don't trust yourself. When panic comes, you have no place to stand. It's as if you're flailing in the middle of an ocean in shark-infested waters. (No offense to sharks.)

Figure 6

- Good values with money
- Trust husband
- Conscientious - about money
- Good problem solver
- I can handle not having everything I want
- Good decision maker
- Good planner
- Mature beyond my years
- Gone through things in the past and got through them
- Responsible
- Like to learn new things
- I care
- I'm thorough
- Stick to commitments
- Stand up for myself
- I know where to find support
- I care about other people's feelings

Connecting with your identity outside fear, like I did with Tally, gives you a *place to stand* and trust yourself. You stand on what is very important to you. Tally's platform was that she cared about people, was interested in learning, was responsible, had creative skills and more. Elevated like this, you can look down at the sea and dangerous water from outside the chaos. It's less scary from up here, and you're now connected with your most important skills that will help you go forward and get yourself on dry land.

You've survived this far and have seen a lot in your life. You've learned a ton and have built up problem-solving skills. You have things in your life that are important to you. Anxiety can't take those away. All it can do is try to pretend that they don't exist. It needs you to believe that, and it's easy to do when the adrenaline is racing through your veins. But they do exist. You can find them and write them down and it will help you remember.

I have seen this practice work thousands of times and used it on myself and my children, too. When you remember what you know, anxiety has a harder time convincing you of its lies. It takes down the intensity of the anxiety, if it comes at all.

Take action

List out your skills and knowledges. During hard or tricky times, what got you through? What have you done in the past when anxiety comes? What are some things that you appreciate about yourself?

_____

_____

_____

_____

_____

_____

_____

Once your list is complete, make a copy and hang one up where you can see it. Carry the other with you throughout your day. (Or take a photo on your phone for easy access.) Read your list twelve times in the morning, twelve times at noon, and twelve times at night. Counting gives it a structure to help your brain take it in. Twelve gives you a goal. It's not so many it becomes tedious, but enough to have it stick.

Remember, it's very important to read through your list when you're feeling calm. I can't stress this enough. Don't wait until you're anxious before pulling out this list. You *can* use it when you're anxious, but only after you've practiced for at least several days when you're calm.

After reading this list so often, these skills are at the top of your mind. When the anxiety comes, they are right there, fresh and clear. You trust them, and so they're nearly impossible to forget. It is such a simple and easy practice that anyone can do. This usually takes less than a minute each time, so being busy is no excuse. (Anxiety takes way too many more precious minutes of your day, so those three minutes are so worth setting aside!)

What do you think? You're amazing, aren't you? You've made it through some major things in your life, and that is nothing short of awesome!

The next chapter will help you understand why you're here in the first place. Most important, you will learn the best thing that you can do for your life — let go of what causes you pain.

Trust the Underdog

You can prevent all of anxiety's dirty tricks and hone every skill in the book, but if you have any doubt, insecurity, feeling of unworthiness or inadequacy, you'll continue to be vulnerable.

There's a reason why you feel inadequate and it's not you. I'll show you how to finally move on from your pain and problems and build a deep trust in yourself that will have you feeling safer and more protected than anything you have tried so far.

Why You Feel Inadequate

The phenomenon of personal failure has grown exponentially over recent decades. Never before has the sense of being a failure to be an adequate person been so freely available to people, and never before has it been so willingly and routinely dispensed. It would now be very rare for me to meet a person in the course of my practice, in the course of my teaching or in the course of my everyday social life, who hasn't experienced, at different times and to different degrees, the specter of personal failure (here I am talking about a sense of inadequacy, incompetence, insufficiency, deficit, backwardness, and so on) looming large in their lives.

~Michael White

I posted this on my Facebook page:[32]

Never forget that you're here for a reason. Your ideas matter and your work in this world makes a difference. The brighter you shine, the more light the world has to live in.

~Marie Forleo
#healnowandforever #youarebeautiful #loveyou

Below it, thirty-five-year-old Gabby commented, "I don't have a reason."

The comment sliced my heart in two. Her words were totally definitive — all limits and no possibility. There's no room for changing her mind. *I don't have a reason. Period. End of story.* I understood that her view of herself and her future is blocked by the wall of blame, shame, fear and guilt. She feels like she's completely failed at life and there is no chance of anything different.

Expectations and pressures we place on ourselves — to be awesome, healed, perfect, young, smart, thin, independent, cool — are increasing in scope and intensity. Not being able to meet these outrageously high personal standards easily convinces us that we're a failure at life — inadequate, deficient and unable. This kind of worry feeds itself, building momentum like a repeating, increasing cycle. You think you are inadequate, you feel bad about yourself, which makes you feel more inadequate, which makes you feel worse about yourself.

You compare yourself to everyone around you, judging yourself harshly, trying to figure out if you are normal. It's not just you who worries you're "not enough," it's a cultural phenomenon. We all grapple with this.

Michel Foucault,[33] a French historian who studied power, found that people behave in ways that we hope will prevent the people around us from excluding or judging us as inadequate. You

---

32 facebook.com/jodiamanlove

might recognize this in your life, feeling like you're in a fishbowl, that everyone is watching you to make sure you are behaving "appropriately." This feeds your insecurities and you isolate yourself to avoid exposing your inadequacies.

I speak from experience. I've felt like everyone was looking at me and judging what they saw. "She doesn't know anything." "She thinks she is funny." "Who does she think she is?" "She is a spaz." "She's crazy." "She's chubby." "She's stupid."

It made me worry how I acted in case I'd inadvertently revealed my shameful inadequacies. My deficiencies felt as visible as a neon sign, no matter how much I tried to fix or hide them. I felt this worry in my whole body and soul. The effects of it were everywhere. I was vulnerable, tired, sad, nervous and felt a deep sense of exclusion. I was not okay. I was different. At the same time, it seemed like I wasn't noticed for what I could do, and this made me feel more invisible and unvalued.

People look at me and assume that I have my life together and that I'm lucky, have a great family, that I'm confident and naturally happy. If you look at me and this makes you feel bad about yourself, listen to me — I looked fine on the outside, even when I didn't feel good on the inside. What people look like on the outside doesn't mean much. Most people hide their pain, insecurities and negative self-judgments. You included. Don't let the *everyone can do it but me* thought destroy your confidence and make you feel

---

33 Michel Foucault, *The Archaeology of Knowledge* (New York: Pantheon Books, 1972). And, Michel Foucault, *Discipline and Punish* (New York: Random House, 1977). Foucault noticed that as opposed to traditional forms of power that are centralized and employed from the top down — like the feudal system — the operation of power we experience in today's world, "Modern Power," goes sideways. He theorized that we control ourselves by perceived assessment by our peers — we think we are in a fishbowl and we act (morally, ethically, and socially) in coherence to a social standard in order to avoid being perceived as different or weird.

more alone. It's simply not true. You are not the only one who feels the way you do. We are all struggling with the same consequences of our cultural expectations. We all have delicate self-esteems.

People create expectations of themselves based on what they think everyone else thinks is right or what they think is supposed to be the right way to be. The biggest problem is that these standards are evasive. "Best" is not definable, so it has you trying to achieve something beyond *best* so you don't miss the mark. You don't know exactly how smart you're supposed to be, so you'd better be extra smart to meet that standard. You're not exactly sure what is perfect, so you aim for beyond perfect to be sure you have it right.

You're setting yourself up for failure with these kinds of unreasonable expectations, so it's tempting to give up. Like Gabby. She feels powerless and hopeless. Her guilt is consuming. So we have to break it down.

Pick Up the Ball

Well, there's a very good reason for staying in the game — there's hope. If you knew that sustaining these standards of perfection takes active participation — it needs you *to believe* you are inadequate — for it to work, then you'd see that you have the power to change it. These expectations oppress you, and within any oppression there is protest. (We talked about this in Trick #9: Anxiety Terrorizes You When You Are Vulnerable.)

Even within the confines of these unrealistic expectations, there have been times where you took the power back and let yourself off the hook, or stood up for the freedom to be who you are and rejoice in being unique. There's also inspiration and support from friends, in blogs, articles, books and on Facebook to reject impractical standards and remind yourself to accept exactly who you are.

You have the skills to disempower these standards and you have the permission.

Sometimes it is safer to see how you have power by looking back on yourself in retrospect. The meme "Letters to my 13-year-old self" is a great example of this. One's power that was so invisible at thirteen is so clearly seen when we look back a few years or even decades later.

Here is my letter to 13-year-old Jodi:

Dear 13-year-old Jodi,

You made it! I almost don't know how you did it given what you are feeling at your age. (That's not true. I believed in you the whole time!) It's inspiring how you kept trusting and searching for answers for how to feel better. Even though you rarely found something that worked, you didn't give up.

This is what I want you to know: You are so much more amazing than you feel like you are. You are kind and observant. You always saw what people needed and were willing to help them. You tried so hard, even though you were tired of being teased, and treated like you were strange and unwelcome. Even though some days you felt like you couldn't stand it another minute. You kept going.

It doesn't matter that your body seems behind the rest of the class. You caught up later. Don't get so down on yourself that you can't write well. You care and that's what's important. This gave you the tenacity to practice and hone your skills. It doesn't matter that you dress like a boy, you figure that out too. Don't listen to what the boys say.

I know our mom told you that boys are mean when they like you. Please know that you don't have to tolerate this. It is never okay for them to be mean. They may have a crush on you and be confused and embarrassed and tease you, but this doesn't mean it's okay. It means you don't have to take it personally. Please don't pay those boys any mind until they learn to get over themselves and treat you with kindness. If they continue to express affection by putting you down, NEVER give them the time of day. And know this has NOTHING to do with you, and does not mean you don't deserve to be treated well.

You are lovely, and worthy, and you will find the love of your life when you get older. You don't have to worry about it too much. Even though you will feel quite passed over for many more years, trust me, it works out great.

There's a lot of things you don't have to worry too much about. You don't have to worry about doing things the right way all the time. There are many ways to do things and you have good, creative ideas. In fact, you are awesome at problem-solving, being motivated and planning. You will be a leader through high school, college and graduate school. And you will help a lot of people during that time.

You don't have to worry about being different. Eventually you will be happy that you are unique. Being silly won't always be embarrassing, but joyful. You don't have to worry about being invisible. You are not invisible. Many people see you and think you are great. You don't see it right now. Sometimes it is hard in the moment. I understand. But you are loved.

I know friendships are hard sometimes. People are hard. They say things that hurt you and don't seem to care. It's mostly because they don't know they've hurt you. They are dealing with their own insecurities and what they say has nothing to do with you. All of your friends are trying hard to figure out their own lives. When they say something mean it is because they need a bit more love.

This doesn't mean be a doormat. You can love them without taking their mean words into your heart. You'll feel better and you might help them, too. That may seem strange to you right now, but you'll understand when you are older.

Please practice giving yourself some compassion. Whatever you are feeling, tell yourself "It's ok, I understand." Allow yourself to feel that because this will keep your sense of yourself intact. You will feel validated and worthy instead of alone.

Little Jodi, you are a cutie-pie! I know you are worried you won't make it, but you can do this. In fact, you will do great things in your life. Subtle, small things, but they will mean the world to a few people. You will save lives by seeing the good in people. You'll learn to celebrate yourself and this will give you energy to do more.

You can trust yourself. Just try it a little for now. And if you have any questions write to me. I'll answer.

Much love,

Older-wiser-happy, Jodi

Thirteen is a highly sensitive age where we're trying to figure out ourselves and our place in the world. In the process of trying very hard to "get it right," we tend to get stressed and down. However, in retrospect, we can clearly see that the standards we thought were important back then, weren't in the long run. If we can do it in retrospect, we can do it now.

While trying to heal yourself of anxiety (or depression, hurt, pain, grief, betrayal), it's essential to feel better about yourself. To do this, you start by stripping away at these outer layers of negative self-judgment from Figure 3 that cause you guilt, shame and doubt.

Figure 3 again.

Black: Original feeling: "Loss"
Grey dotted: Negative self-judgments
Striped: Fears and anxieties
Black dotted: Secondary layer of negative self-judgments

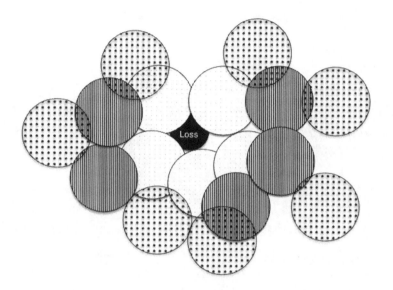

To do this, I find it helpful to understand guilt. The guilt and shame we carry (the dotted circles) seem true, because those cultural expectations seem true. We think we deserve it, so we hold on to it. But this is not how guilt is supposed to work.

Guilt is an emotion like fear. It comes with being human. Fear has a biological purpose, it gets the body ready to take action to protect itself from danger. Guilt has an emotional purpose — to call your attention to something that doesn't feel right. With this consciousness you can respect the situation. "Re" and "spect" means to look again. From here, you can make a decision on what to do next. Apologize. Reach out to someone. Fix something. Give back. Show appreciation. Acknowledge someone. Repair. Or simply commit to doing something different the next time.

Guilt is an invitation to take action. Just like the biological fear response. With fear, when you take action, the fear becomes useless and since the energy has gone into the action, it goes away. Guilt is the same. Once the action is decided, the guilt is useless and can dissipate.

The problem in our culture is that people get trapped in the guilt, because those dotted circles make us feel like a failure. They are heavy and zap energy. Instead of taking action and letting go of guilt, people keep the guilt and don't act. It's just like anxiety. (Remember: Anxiety is the leftover fear when you are not in a dangerous situation. It makes people feel stuck, immobilized and helpless.)

Getting unstuck is the trick to feeling better. You have to both lower the outrageous expectations you have about yourself and learn how to employ guilt in the way it's meant to work.

Deborah

Deborah, who had lived through a long and abusive first marriage, came to see me for counseling four years after she managed to escape. She wanted help with what she described as "kinesthetic flashbacks" — a feeling of sickness in her body when a memory of her ex-husband was evoked. She worried that she was suffering from what she called "irrational fears." I asked her for some examples.

"If I go to the mall, I'm irrationally afraid I might run into him [her ex-husband]. I think he might be there watching me from a distance. I scan the parking lot as I walk in to see if he's lurking. And also, when I come home from work each night, I pull into my garage, but stay in my car with the doors locked until my garage door goes all the way down."

She tells me with the expectation that I'll consider these precautions insane. I blink. I tell her I'm still waiting for the irrational fear, since I haven't heard one yet. She offers no more examples.

"What makes these irrational?" I ask.

She tells me that her friends, family and a former therapist told her that she should stop worrying. *They told her, You are safe. He has moved on to another woman. You don't have to worry anymore.* This did nothing to sway her anxiety, dispel her fears or curb her flashbacks. Instead, this reinforced her growing self-judgment about being irrational or crazy.She said, "If I was normal, I would stop worrying."

This idea crippled her self-confidence and dwindling trust in her ability to protect herself, which amplified her anxiety. During our conversation, I learned what supported her fears. When she left, her ex had told her, "I'll come for you. Years from now, when you're relaxed and no longer expect me to. That's when I will come and hurt you for leaving me."

We talked about her skills and imagined how they would give her the advantage, if anything happened. We decided her skills, which we named "Skills to be alert and aware of her surrounding," were necessary, courageous and admirable. We noticed the significance of her being able to go out at all. We acknowledged that these protective skills weren't hurting anybody and barely took any extra time out of her day. The skills weren't a problem; the way she thought about them was the only issue. Seeing them as intelligent changed how she felt about herself and decreased her anxiety and flashbacks.

Feeling inadequate is the backbone of anxiety decreasing your trust in yourself. When you don't trust our own competency, you feel out of control. Fear and anxiety take hold.

Three Steps to Emotional Freedom

1. Have self-compassion
2. Take a step back
3. Let go

Here are stories and explanations to help implement them in your life.

Have self-compassion

I don't understand why I feel this way, I thought. I'm doing all the right things. I know how to feel better but I'm still panicking. I should be better by now. Oh no! I just can't do it. I don't get it.

These thoughts came through my mind a million times. At the same time I had a deep desire for someone to understand. Partly so they could explain it to me, but also because that would mean they'd get it — and get "me" — and I wouldn't feel so terribly alone all the time. The desperate loneliness made me feel unloved and unworthy of love.

Because I felt like nobody understood — a reflection of me not understanding — it put me in the position of defending my anxiety. *You don't understand, it's really bad. I can't do it. I'm too anxious!*

It was as if I was defending my visibility. If nobody understood me, I would be invisible, and that equals unworthiness. *Explaining is the only way to hold on to my worth,* I mistakenly thought. But the more I defended, the worse I felt, the more confused I got, the more isolated I became, the more I judged myself harshly, the more I gave anxiety power. Again in the guise of protecting myself, I caused myself more intense suffering.

Back then, when someone in my life showed me some under-standing, my negativity would temporarily melt away. I would be filled with warmth! It freed me from having to defend my problems. And this freedom shifted something in me. I no longer had to hold tightly to my problems for my sense of self-worth to stay intact. I was loved and my problems had less hold on me.

It would be great if I always had someone there to give me understanding when I needed reassurance. Though I received this sometimes, my own negative self-judgment would take over, eventually undoing the love and making me feel out in the cold again. The problem was that I didn't have any compassion for myself and my feelings.

I didn't allow them at all, thinking that allowing my feelings meant I had to tolerate them. Panic was awful; I'd rather die than tolerate it. My whole focus and attention was set on avoiding it. But this caused more problems.

When something negative happens, stories fly through our head — stories about what happened, why it happened, whose fault it was, and more. In a way, these stories keep us from having to *feel*. Instead of feeling, we're figuring it all out, making meaning around it, trying to make it have sense and obsessing over it. Or you can ignore the problem, avoid it and fill yourself up with other things that falsely promise you a sense of worth like unfulfilling relationships, food, video games or drugs. These help you escape having to feel, but you find out sooner or later that these are empty promises. Temporary solutions masking — yet increasing — the problem.

These stories keep you suffering. You fear consequences, lament your past, judge your responses, blame others for hurting you, blame yourself for driving them to it. This fills your head, causing greater worry and stress. It's like worry on top of worry and judgment on top of judgment. (See Figure 3.)

This increases the fear response and you feel terrible physically, emotionally and mentally. The stories about the feelings and what happened to bring about those feelings — blaming yourself and blaming others — fill your head and don't allow you to feel. They are the opposite of self-compassion. This is what takes so long to heal. You may think a feeling is unbearable, yet you're willing to endure years of self-torture with stories of blame, fear and guilt cluttering your mind.

People spend so much of their lives running away from feelings, thinking that they will hurt. You think that facing loneliness, shame or worthlessness would be completely overwhelming. That comes with your thoughts and stories, not your feelings. Look again at the circles (Figure 3). It's not the small black "Loss" that knocks you to your knees, it is the dotted negative self-judgments and the striped fears that make you feel overwhelmed. And as long as you run away from the small black in life, the big dotted and striped circles will continue to torment you. An unfelt, unresolved feeling, especially one you judge to be pathological, can wreak havoc on your emotions, your relationships and your identity. You might not be feeling, but it *feels* like you are, since you're suffering so badly.

One of the most powerful ways to express self-compassion is by allowing yourself to feel the small black circle without fear and judgment. When we allow ourselves to feel without the story — just feel — it can go away. *Women, Food, and God* author Geneen Roth says, "If you don't start a feeling, you cannot take that feeling to an end." If you don't feel, you're cheating yourself of the relief of finishing it. In a way, the feeling is chasing you, merely one step behind, keeping you moving, fighting and existing in a perpetual state of stress since you can't let down your guard in case it catches up. However, if you allow yourself to feel it, it's never as bad as you assumed. The running is so much worse. You may have thought you were protecting yourself, but you're just causing more suffering.

The reason you and I have balked at gurus saying "just let go of hurt feelings" is again because this sounds invalidating. It makes us feel stupid for having them or like we're overreacting and it didn't matter. Or that we're unworthy of deserving better treatment. We worry that if we move on, it never mattered what someone *did*.

It's not your job to suffer so that someone stays accountable. It doesn't work that way. If anything, if you continue to suffer, the person who hurt you gets to keep power. Read this post that Antoine Leiris wrote on Facebook just days after his wife was murdered in the terrorist attacks in Paris on November 13, 2015.

Friday night you stole the life of an exceptional being, the love of my life, the mother of my son, but you won't have my hatred. I do not know who you are and I don't want to know. You're dead souls. If this God for whom you kill blindly made us in His own image, every bullet in my wife's body would have been a wound in His heart.

Therefore, I will not give you the gift of hating you. You have obviously sought it, but responding to it with anger would be to give in to the same ignorance that has made you who you are. You want me to be afraid? To cast a mistrustful eye on my fellow citizens? To sacrifice my freedom for security? You lost. Same player. Same game.

I saw her this morning, finally, after many nights and days of waiting. She was just as beautiful as she was when she left on Friday evening. As beautiful as when I fell madly in love with her more than 12 years ago. Of course I'm devastated with grief, I will give you that tiny victory. But this will be a short-term grief. I know she will join us every day and that we will find each other again in the paradise of free souls which you will never have access to.

We are only two, my son and I, but we are more powerful than all world's armies. In any case, I have no more time to waste on you. I need to get back to Melvil who is just waking up from his nap. He is just 17 months old; he'll eat his snack like every day, then we are going to play like we do every day. And every day of his life this little boy will insult you with his happiness and freedom. Happy and free. Because you don't have his hatred either.[34]

Feeling your feelings is totally different. It helps you feel validated and worthy. This is how you do it — you have to allow yourself to feel your feelings without judgment and have compassion instead.

Many, many years ago, I was terribly hurt by being left out of a family event. Nobody meant to do it and thus didn't understand my hurt. This made me feel unacknowledged and worse. I went into another room, lay on the bed and spilled tears of loneliness and unworthiness for a good hour. At first, I hated myself for overreacting and causing a scene. Then, I allowed myself to be hurt. I loved myself through it — without judgment. The story unraveled and I realized I was hurt because it was important to me to be kind and inclusive of others. I acknowledged myself for being kind and inclusive and appreciated myself for those traits. This gave me value. My tears dried up and I felt so much better.

Your sadness, fear, pain, grief is a human response to an event. You are human. You may feel like you ought to be more spiritually evolved than to ever let something human bother you, but that negative judgment is just keeping you stuck. Compassion is about loving yourself through every little thing you think and feel. Everything belongs. Every feeling is allowed. When you feel something, practice saying, "I understand why I feel this way," or "I get it."

Judging something gives it attention and makes it crave more attention. When you "get it," it doesn't need an ounce more of your time and it dissolves.

---

34 Translated from French to English by BBC News.

Take action

Read the following guided imagery and find yourself a quiet space to sit and close your eyes to try it.

Think about a feeling, the raw feeling, not the story — not judgment, blame, regret — just the feeling. For this short period of time you are going to suspend the story about it. Imagine that feeling in your body somewhere and see it as if it is a shape, image or color. (Like a thick black cloud over your heart, or a rock in your stomach.) Pretend you are sitting in a folding chair watching yourself with this feeling-shape in you. You are witnessing this shape in your body and feeling the feeling, without the story: You see and feel the shape, but you don't know what it means. (If the story comes back in your mind, that's okay. Gently and compassionately let it go and go back to feeling and observing the raw feeling.)

Now, breathe into that shape. Take five long, slow breaths. Then, check in with yourself and notice if anything has changed. Don't assess, just notice. Then, repeat the process: five long breaths. Imagine that air coming into and around that shape. Again, stop to notice any changes. Continue this until the shape changes, becomes benign, transformed, or is completely dissolved. This may take three to thirty minutes.[35]

This practice has changed my life. I use it again and again whenever I'm struggling. I've also taught it to people who have been amazed by the results, resolving feelings in a matter of minutes they've been running away from for years.

Discontent breeds discontent. This is because if you constantly think you should be somewhere else, then you hold yourself accountable as if it's your fault you're not there. If you are struggling with anxiety, I understand why you don't like how you feel.

---

35   Find my free audio version of this online: jodiaman.com/you1anxiety0

But if you stop being discontented and start being compassionate, everything will change.

Figuring out how to think about yourself and your problems is one of the most important things you can do for yourself. A mantra I use to be more compassionate with myself is, "You are exactly where you are supposed to be." I say this no matter what I feel — this compassion takes away the chaos of shame, clearing the way for me to navigate through and make sense of the situation. Now I can get some distance from what happened and view it from outside the chaos.

Take a step back

I was sitting on the edge of my tub, my body wracked with sobs with heart-wrenching rejection digging into my soul. I felt so alone. Reaching out to my friends, hoping someone would understand how I felt, I received this advice: "Jodi, you can't take it personally."

But I was so deep into feeling like a victim that this advice made me worse. It was a double whammy! Not only was I rejected, but I "wasn't handling it right."

"Don't take it personally" is excellent advice, but when someone is upset like I was they're not yet in the place to hear it. It felt like my pain was invalidated and it didn't matter that someone hurt me. This made me defend my pain because, in a way, it felt like I was defending my worth as a person. And so I held on to that pain more tightly. I was too deep in the chaos of my rejection to see anything else.

This is how I learned that compassion has to come first. The compassion settles the chaos. It's then we're able to take a step back from the situation and get a perspective from outside the intense hurt and emotions.

Taking a step back is like looking at a situation from an outsider view, as if you are not emotionally involved. I've also heard this called "above the battlefield." When I do this, I imagine myself seeing the situation from above and looking at all the players in the situation as if they were little characters acting out the scene. No longer distracted by our emotions and our story of victimization, this perspective changes our taken-for-granted beliefs about a situation, our role and our identity. It clarifies how to move forward. To do this practice, all you need is to give yourself some time.

When something happens, before you react, take a moment for yourself. Sometimes I even excuse myself to the bathroom to give myself a few minutes. There I close my eyes and spend a minute in my imagination witnessing the scene.

One day, after having compassion for myself and pulling myself back from a small frustrating situation, a difficult phone call that caused me more work, I understood what happened and why I had taken it so personally. I wrote on Facebook as a reminder to what I discovered, "I am only a victim when I think I am" — something I only recognized, because I showed myself some compassion and took a step back. Proclaiming this publicly was a ritual to solidify my commitment to no longer let the phone conversation take energy from my day. It worked. I felt better.

I also hoped to inspire my Facebook community by sharing this lesson with them. Shortly thereafter, I received this message.

When you say, "I am only a victim when I think I am," doesn't that involve guilt? If something bad happens and I'm not a victim, then I had what I deserved? That is how I read it, but I know it's certainly not what you mean.

If I was walking in the street and a man comes and stabs me to death, how can I not be a victim unless I think I am? What would I be? Guilty for walking in the street?

She was right. According to my dictionary a victim is a "(noun) Unfortunate person who suffers from some adverse circumstance." Or "(noun) A person who is tricked or swindled." No one ever deserves to be a victim.

The concept of victim mentality uses "victim" as a metaphor to suggest one is a victim of his or her thoughts. Victim mentality can be when you're a victim of the way you make meaning out of situations that can cause greater suffering. This can look like many different things. For example, you can be sad, angry or scared and then on top of that, your *mind* can worry and judge those feelings and make conclusions on what they say about you. So the original feeling is the black circle and the victim mentality makes it worse (The dotted and striped circles in Figure 3).

If you were walking down the street and someone stabbed you, you would be the literal victim in that situation, but if you took that on as a permanent identity, it would affect how you think, how you feel and how you behave thereafter. It would be like taking the stabbing personally, when it really happened because of the perpetrator's problems. That would give the attacker continued power to make you feel vulnerable.

This is how victim mentality works. You might notice that people are not listening, taking advantage, ignoring, disrespecting or leaving you. Then victim mentality has you making conclusions around your identity because of it. *I am a loser. Nobody loves me. Or, I can't do anything right.*

When we think that everyone is against us and no one understands, most things — even well-intentioned things — can sound like criticism and judgment. This is directly related to us judging ourselves. If we didn't judge ourselves, nobody would judge us or we wouldn't notice it if someone did. We'd hear their comments differently or not hear them at all. Our mindset exacerbates problems, just like "not feeling your feelings" does. These thoughts and beliefs — especially while they hold a truth status in your mind — cannot help but make you feel worse.

When you realize that you have power over a situation, you can go one of two ways. You can either be relieved that you can do something or alternatively judge or defend yourself. That is your choice. On some level, knowing you can do something about your problems can bring you freedom. *What relief! I have control! I can do something about this!* But instead it often brings defensiveness and judgment. Defensiveness comes because you feel invalidated. It's a sign that you know you're worthy — which is good — however, defensiveness makes you validate your problems instead of validating yourself, so it makes you *feel* worse.

We blame ourselves for not being able to figure out how to heal. One client told me, "Elizabeth Gilbert [author of *Eat, Pray, Love*] can go off meds, but I can't." Or people often say, "If it's my choice to be happy, I must be doing something wrong." We think we're too stupid to figure out how (since everyone else can), or it makes us want to blame others who hurt or betrayed us.

The fix is to take a step back. You can't change having been a victim, but you can change how you think about what is happening or what happened. Postpone creating meaning until you've taken time out and gotten distance from the situation. Whether it's for a minute or a few days, you'll be able to employ these four important benefits.

1. Time to get beyond the knee-jerk response.
2. Ability to not take things personally.
3. Freedom from doubt's influence.
4. Clear vision of your choice.

1. Time to get beyond the knee-jerk response.

When I get a message, email or phone call that rubs me the wrong way, I want to stop everything and spend an hour writing a scathing response. There's a bit of pleasure for me to come up with the right words to put that idiot in their place. My knee-jerk fantasy response is vicious when I'm scorned.

There have been times in the past when I made that fantasy a reality and responded in this heightened emotional state. It usually doesn't go well. So now I take some time before responding and I usually find that after a few hours or a few days, I may not need to respond at all.

2. Ability to not take things personally.

The world is unfair. Much of it is random — you hit a lot of red lights, get a bad cold, the package you ordered is late or someone didn't do what they promised. Things go wrong. Big things and little things.

If it is someone else hurting you, their actions say more about them than they do you. Again, people are not mean to you because they don't like you — they are mean to you because they don't like themselves. Their misery is so huge that it bubbles over onto the people around them. If they're judgmental, it's because they are judging themselves harshly.

What tempts us to take things personally is our mind trying to figure out why something happened and self-blame being the easiest answer.

When a lot of things happen to you, you might be tempted to conclude it's *you*, because you're the most common denominator. You got messages in the past that it's your fault someone was mean to you, but that was just their tactic of power. It is not about you. None of it.

Life's isn't always easy. Bad things happen to good people. You don't have to blame yourself for the world. When you see a situation from above the battlefield, you see why other people do what they did. You'll see the pain, fear and confusion on their part that had them acting out and feel how badly they're judging themselves. You'll see that their issues have nothing to do with you.

You'll also comprehend what was triggered in you. You'll witness your knee-jerk response and have compassion for it. You can understand what you're defending and realize that thing is very precious to you. Then, you can honor yourself for holding that precious thing, stand taller and feel better.

You no longer feel the need to retaliate, because the person who hurt you just seems like a very sad soul. And even if you decide to respond, you'll be clear on the consequences of that response so you don't do anything that you'll regret or that will cause you more pain. You'll be able to respond from your higher wisdom.

3. Freedom from doubt's influence.

Doubt is pervasive. It also comes from those impossibly high standards that you *doubt* you can meet. Unsure if you're adequate, you analyze yourself and find evidence from past mistakes and problems to prove you can't trust yourself. The chaos of a difficult situation is a perfect Petri dish for doubt to grow in.

When you take a step back, you break through this chaos and doubt deflates.

Humans are meaning makers. After each experience we have, we go through a mental process deciding what it means to us. This meaning is highly influenced by our previous understandings about ourselves and the world. When something difficult happens to us, we experience it as chaotic and our mind wants to make sense of it. People crave order.

Nature *is* chaotic. If a person is left in the woods under a pine tree for a few hours, something interesting happens. He or she begins to line up sticks by width, balance rocks in a cairn or make a little seat of soft moss. This is because people crave order, and this person begins creating order in their small patch of wilderness.

Abuse, betrayal and rejection are chaotic to the psyche. They seem "unnatural" and nonsensical. When you experience them, the fastest way to create order is blame, so you would go there first. Sometimes you blame yourself and sometimes you blame someone else, but mostly you're going back and forth blaming yourself and the other person. *Is it me or is it them? Is it me or is it them?*

Doubt ensues, creating a conflict in your mind that causes much more suffering. You attempt to find order and end up creating more chaos. Taking a step back helps you to see the doubt as another player in the scene. You understand the situation and doubt has less power. You can address it directly.

Doubt, I know it is you. You are trying to make me think all these things and you tell me that these things mean something, but it is just you trying to trick me. Have a seat, I am busy right now.

(Doubt is a very serious dude and this makes you believe it, so it's best to be light and silly when talking to it. See Skill #12: Lighten Up.)

4. Clear vision of your choice.

When you take a step back, you have clarity on how to move forward.

Some people say, *Everything happens for a reason.* This isn't something I believe. "Everything happens for a reason" suggests you have to embrace the bad thing. Forget doing that. There is no reason to do that. You know it sucked.

It's much more complicated than that anyway. Things happen and you have no choice but to go forward.

Embrace your skills in moving forward. It's inevitable that you learn and experience things on the way, which can be a positive consequence of that horrible thing. You don't have to be glad you went through that horrible time, but you can still appreciate the benefits. In doing this, you decrease the negative consequences of that experience.

There's a fable of a man who served in prison for thirty years. He had two sons. One son went on to have a successful career in business, be a contributing member of his local community and raise a well-loved family. The other son led a life of crime, stealing and cheating the system, and ended up in prison himself. When both boys were asked what most influenced their life's path, both of them said, "My father."

Your response to life can affect you in good ways or bad ways. That is your choice. Embrace the actions you took and what these say about what's important to you. You can forgive, forget, stop thinking, stop worrying, let something go, have compassion, be creative, survive, connect, listen, learn, grow, protect and more. Keep in mind, within every oppression, there is a protest. This protest says something about you. It might say you are courageous, thoughtful, intelligent, a good problem solver, creative and caring. This is always more important than the oppression.

When you take a step back, the action you want to take becomes clear. You can think about how it will play out and adjust to how you want things to be. And go forward knowing you might not get the response from others that you desire, and not feel bad about that — since you can see why they weren't able to give that to you.

Let go

In fact, not forgiving is like drinking rat poison
and then waiting for the rat to die.

~Anne Lamott

It's time to give you the steps to finally let go of blame, doubt, shame and guilt. Yes!

But first, let me honor you for making it this far in the book. Not many people would be so committed as to finish a book on this fraught, painful and personal topic. You are doing awesome! Way to commit and keep going!

It means something that you've continued reading. It means you won't let anything stop you from feeling better. You've wanted to let go for a long time, and now you're showing up for the answer to how. I'm so glad you're still with me. I will deliver, but this is where the practicing gets a bit more intense. It's not hard and it isn't painful — it's just remembering to practice. Once you let go, the self-love[36] will come in. It's already there, I promise you, but the fear, blame and guilt have been blocking it.

It's time to stop that inner battle of the blame game — that war raging in your head, keeping you stuck. *Is it me? Is it him? Is it me? Is it him?* STOP! There's nothing for you there. With no resolution, your torment will continue. You can end up feeling like a wrung-out piece of rag and hating yourself. This conflict is so distracting and limits you from possibilities, relationships and opportunities for joy and fun in your life. You don't need this hell anymore. Let's resolve it and end that conflict right now. This is what you do: You have to consciously decide once and for all the meaning of the past hurts that are troubling you so your mind stops asking. It's best to keep this simple. Try using this template.

"_____ *happened. It was not okay. I did not deserve it. But it doesn't have to define me anymore.*"

Let me explain each piece of that and why it is important.

_____ *happened.*

Your acknowledgment that it happened builds trust and confidence in yourself. Many people question whether some-

---

36   Videos on self-love: jodiaman.com/you1anxiety0.

thing awful actually happened since it's so crazy that someone (the abuser/betrayer) would act that way. Memories become foggy when there's trauma, and we question whether it really occurred. This is just another way our minds get stuck. Decide that it happened.

It was not okay.

This is a rich acknowledgement that something untoward happened and also contributes to a more robust sense of self by expressing that it was horrible. It validates *you*, not what happened to you. This dissolves you of the responsibility of *allowing yourself* to be hurt or somehow bringing it onto yourself.

I did not deserve it.

Deserve is such a sticky word. Bad and good things happening is not connected to what you deserve. Bad things happen to good people, good things happen to mean people. What happens to us has nothing to do with our worth, but we've been conditioned to attach these things together. Saying *I did not deserve it* settles the question of blame. If you blame yourself for something someone else did, taking into your heart that you didn't deserve what happened to you will heal your soul and restore your worth as a human being and as a spiritual being.

It doesn't have to define me.

Events are not your identity. Events happen. You are made up of what is important to you, not what happened to you. So often when people make meaning out of atrocities, this translates to how they see themselves. This is never helpful and causes most of our human suffering.

If you feel troubled about a past event when you know you've made a mistake, you can make a conscious meaning out of this, too.

"_____ *happened. I did it. It was not okay. I have and will continue to restore the relationship/my community. It doesn't have to define me anymore.*"

Here's the explanation to this.

_____ *happened. I did it. It was not okay.*

You acknowledge your responsibility to whom it may have hurt. You leave the excuses behind; there's no *but* or *because*.

I have and will continue to restore the relationship/my community.

You state your commitment and stand accountable. You value the feelings of those you offended.

It doesn't have to define me anymore.

It's an action you took, but it isn't who you are. You can have compassion that you are human and make mistakes. Your past doesn't define you — how you want to be does. Holding on to it doesn't help the person you hurt, it just poisons you.

Either way, you have to decide that's the meaning you're going to keep about the event and let all of the questions go. Decide that you no longer need to search for answers, because you're all set.

When you define yourself by the bad things you did, you think you did, or that others did to you, you feel separate and unworthy. This never feels good. You are not these things. These things happened, but they don't define you. They don't have to pin you to the ground anymore.

Most people don't know how to forgive or let go. They want to and try, but still feel bad. This is because besides the intention of forgiving, you have to reprogram your mind. Changing beliefs takes practice, but it is simple.

Here are the essential steps to letting go.
- Decide you deserve it
- Set the intention
- Practice

1. Decide you deserve it.

You can decide to let something go whether you're responsible or not. It's about having compassion for yourself, which is an understanding about why you feel the way you do or acted the way you did. It doesn't condone or excuse it to understand you did it, because you were confused, made a mistake, under the influence, misguided, acted impulsively or were in pain.

If someone did something to you, you deserve to heal from it. People all over the place can hurt us, annoy us, betray us, ignore us, humiliate us, abuse us and degrade us. It's not ever okay that they do that. Even if this has happened many times in your life, this doesn't mean you deserve it. Remember, people who hurt you don't like themselves. Don't be surprised that a *lot* of people have hurt you — it's because a *lot* of people don't like themselves. You have no control over them. You can only control you, and you have to let the hurt into your heart for it to bother you.

Read this quote by Marlene Marlow.

"All new encounters are tests — with food, with people, with ideas. Smell everything first. If someone tells you something, smell it! If it smells alright, then try a little for the taste, but always chew it. Chew for a long time before you swallow. Even words should be chewed for a long time before swallowing because it is easier to spit something out than it is to get rid of it once you have already taken it in."

As a young therapist in training, I sat in on a session between a woman and my supervisor. She was immobilized by depression which affected her career, her relationships and her financial independence. As he asked about her life, he externalized the thoughts in her head into two categories, "Deserving Thoughts" and "Not-Deserving Thoughts." As we uncovered her daily thoughts, he listed them in the appropriate columns. There was a gross imbalance favoring Not-Deserving Thoughts that, as it turned out, sabotaged any effort she made toward creating a life she wanted.

Listening, I realized I could categorize my own thoughts this way, too. Each of us secretly feels undeserving, but hopes upon hope that we're seen as deserving. It's a lot of pressure and stress trying to figure out our worth.

I feel honored every day that I get to witness my clients' shift in their self-worth from undeserving to deserving, first in small ways and then in big ways. This negative self-image comes from the past. It's often the voice of someone who should have been trustworthy — a parent, an uncle, a grandparent. But instead this person told them that they were stupid and not good enough in speech and in action every chance they got. The voice stays with people, long past the end of the abuser's life, and it's hard to get rid of. It defines for them who they are and what their position in the world is — loser, disgusting, subhuman, undeserving.

When this kind of verbal degrading is combined with physical and/or sexual abuse, it's worse, because people blame themselves for the abuse they received. Compounding the problem, they think they're unworthy of forgiveness.

Your lack of worth holds that truth status in your mind, because of so-called evidence you've built up from your past, but this evidence is false and is often quite thin. *I made a bad choice.*

I allowed it to happen. It must be me. People hold on to something, because it seems it would make them less important if they let it go. Or we hold on to it just so the other person can be held accountable. Or maybe we're awaiting validation.

You do deserve to feel valued and respected. You also deserve that the other person feels bad for hurting you. You also deserve validation for your pain. *You deserve!* But staying miserable to prove this is only hurting you. You must decide for yourself that you're worthy of healing, letting go of the past and forgiving yourself so you can move on with your life.

Having self-compassion is the key to having self-tolerance. Being understanding instead of rigid and judgmental with yourself is the quickest way to find your deserving self.

2. Set the intention.

The second step of letting go is easy. This is as simple as stating or thinking the intention or commitment. You can say, "I can let this guilt go," when you're talking about something you did or "I don't want to hold this anymore, I will let go."

A ceremony or ritual can help sustain this commitment you're making. For example, go sit by some water and find a rock, blow into that rock all of the hurt and bad feelings and old beliefs, then throw the rock into the water. The ritual creates rich meaning, putting a vital energy around your commitment to let go. This will help sustain it.[37]

3. Practice.

This third step is what many people haven't learned, but it's the most important. You don't let go, you *practice* letting go. Literally.

---

37   Check out my video about this: "How to let go of pain and problems." jodia-man.com/let-go-pain-problems

You build your skills by practicing them.

Keep in mind that even though you're spiritually and emotionally evolving, you're still human. Your mind will do what the mind does — continue to question. Expect the feelings of resentment, fear, guilt and anger to come back. They've been a habit for a long time and have their own power outside your intention to let them go. Them coming back doesn't mean you didn't do it right or are messed up. This is what happens to everybody. It would be weirder still if they did *not* come back.

This is where the practicing comes in.

As soon as you've noticed those thoughts come into your mind, stay light. The more you take them seriously and get frustrated, the worse you'll feel. If you judge them or yourself you will just be giving them loads of attention and energy, attaching yourself to the suffering.

Instead, use this practice. With great self-compassion say,

"Hello, guilt. I knew you would come back. I decided that I don't need you anymore. Have a seat, I'm busy right now."

You will have to do this over and over. *Over and over!* As you practice this without judgment and with total compassion, the negative feeling will begin to come less often.

Lots of self-care activities will help with this process, especially daily meditation, movement, creative pursuits, friendships and deep breathing that will relax your mind. Remember, if you stop judging — you let go.

Having self-compassion, taking a step back and letting go are the keys to healing your life, feeling better about yourself and eliminating anxiety. If you make these easy practices the priority in your life, you'll never experience loneliness, betrayal, anxiety or doubt in the same way again. Instead you will be filled with confidence and compassion for yourself and others, which will give you peace in your heart and a lightness in your soul. You'll be able to create the life you want and handle what comes your way by loving, staying connected and by solidly trusting yourself.

You for the Win

How do you nurture a positive attitude
when all the statistics say you're a dead man?
You go to work.
~Patrick Swayze

I hope you've come to understand that the answer to relieving anxiety is not singular. Practicing letting go of guilt and anxiety keeps you feeling safe and gives you the energy you need to generate happiness in your days. Calling anxiety out on its lies and developing your skills help you trust yourself and feel in control. Retraining the unnecessary triggers of your amygdala stops unwanted automatic panic response. And transforming beliefs affects how you experience your future.

Your beliefs influence how you understand the world. Some are great and helpful, and others limit your recovery, relationships and potential. Thankfully, they're not permanent. The easiest way to change an unwanted belief is by using affirmations.

An affirmation is an intention or positive belief focusing on a preferred outcome. When your mind is hurting you by repeating the negative beliefs, you can use affirmations to repeat how you want to think of yourself. Practicing affirmations can change the way you think by subjugating the negative and breathing life into the preferred message about yourself. After a period of practicing affirmations, the new empowered, positive self-talk becomes the go-to belief instead of the negative self-critic. Strategic affirmations can permanently change, turn down or eliminate the negative voices in your head.

You may have tried affirmations such as "I am light" or "I am love" in the past. They can help you feel relaxed and put you in a meditative state. They give you strength to have more patience and stamina to resist your problematic thinking, but this doesn't give you the big change you're looking for.

You can look in the mirror and say, "I love you. You're the greatest!" all day, every day. But if you don't believe the words, it doesn't help. Affirmations have to be believed for them to work. This might be confusing, because first I'm saying to use affirmations to change beliefs, and then I'm saying you have to already believe them for them to work.

Saying, "I love you. You're the greatest!" could make you feel more confident and steady in that belief each day — unless you don't believe that you're lovable at all. Then the affirmation would remain out of touch even if you said it a zillion times. That's because you're jumping too fast to the new identity. There's too big a gap between what you think now and what you *want* to think. The best way to close that gap is to do it gradually.

Because of that old story of yourself, the guilt, shame, self-blame and fear have built up a huge case against you, flinging disparaging thoughts your way. If you try to change your thinking about this too fast, shame will retaliate, making you feel worse by asking, "How dare you be so selfish and egotistical as to think you are lovable?"

Not only do these affirmations fail to work, but they may make you feel even more alone in the world and up against too much.

Then you judge yourself harshly, because everyone can do affirmations but you. You feel like a failure *again*.

Don't despair. The reason those affirmations don't get rid of your anxiety is not you. And you're not alone. It's because there is too big a gap between your dominant story of pain and self-loathing, to the preferred story of joy and self-compassion.

I use stepping-stone affirmations to transverse the gap.

To write an affirmation that works, you first have to identify a belief that you want to change, such as, "I will never get better." Then, name the place you would like to get to, "I will get better." Next, write a series of affirmations beginning with something you do believe and getting closer and closer to your desired belief.

When you're ready to write your own affirmations, make sure you have a notebook. Writing down your affirmations improves the impact this has on your life.[38] Say your affirmations out loud too, because it helps to shift your mind and infuse your memory. Changing your brain is just like any other learning process. Repetition is important. Say and read your affirmation at least three times a day, twelve times per session. (Examples below.)

Take notes after you repeat the affirmation. Write down the percentage of how much you fully embrace that new belief. And write down any evidence you have for this to be true. The day you get to one hundred percent, you take the next step and write a new affirmation. Try to feel the affirmation in your body or picture it in your head.

Using affirmations is how I got over my fear of flying. After suffering through seven months of panic, I learned about affirmations six weeks before my trip to Australia. I began practicing right away and within two weeks, I was calm and looking forward to an adventure.

---

38   T.W. James et al., "Multisensory perception of action in posterior temporal and parietal cortices," *Journal of Neuropsychologia* 10 (2010):1016.

Three times a day, I pictured myself calm and happy on a plane. I created an image for myself to focus on where I was sitting in a plane seat and laughing out loud and feeling very calm. Then, whenever my fear of flying was triggered, I conjured up the same image. It worked. I stopped panicking about flying and I spent the last weeks before my trip relaxed and excited.

The plane trip went great. I created the positive experience by imagining it. During one flight I watched my first episode of the TV show, *The Office*, and I actually laughed out loud.

I've repeated this process over and over with myself and others. When I'm worried over being anxious at a function, I picture myself calm and happy there. When children are afraid of panicking in school, I have them counter the vision in their heads of them freaking out in class by replacing the images with scenes of themselves being calm and comfortable.

Make sure the affirmations are targeting what you need. For example, once someone wrote to me because she was afraid of going into knee surgery. She was doing "affirmations" — picturing herself walking on the beach a few months after the surgery. She did this all the time, but still felt horribly anxious, so it wasn't working.

I asked her what she was afraid of and she explained being frightened of the recovery room immediately after surgery. She was terrified of being numb from the anesthesia and feeling trapped and out of control. We reworked her affirmations to target the recovery room feelings. I instructed her to picture herself in the recovery room feeling numb, but being calm and at ease. I asked her to do these affirmations kinesthetically by imagining that calmness in her body.

Later, she told me that doing this shifted things in a major way, eliminating her constant panic. I wasn't surprised. The new affirmations were specific to her fears.

Think specific, doable steps. Don't worry about trying to do it fast. Work up to the affirmations that feel overwhelming or not quite believable. Small steps keep you efficiently moving and feeling successful. Then, commit to doing your affirmations. Don't decide too quickly that they don't work. Be flexible. If they're not working, look at what other limiting beliefs may be in the way and take care of those first.

Examples of Affirmations That Work

Current belief: *I can't get better.*

Desired belief: *I will get better.*

Create the first affirmation describing something you can believe, even if it just barely.

First affirmation: *There may be, however small and remote, a possibility that I can get better even though I don't see it right now.*

Say this first affirmation twelve times, three times a day. Program it into your phone as a reminder. Discipline yourself not to shortcut this process. This is an effort, but it's the easiest thing you'll do all day. Don't dismiss it *because* it's too easy. It works!

Repeat this until you believe it fully. Then write another one.

Second affirmation: *There might be a possibility that I can get better.*

Say that one twelve times, three times a day for as many days, weeks or months as you need to feel it and believe it all the way into your heart. Just keep it up until you believe it absolutely and fully.

Remember, don't get distressed about how much time it takes. That just invites judgment. The more compassion and the less judgment you have, the better.

Write the next affirmation.

Third affirmation: *I may be better. I think I can get better.*

Say that as long as you need to. Then make a slight shift. Fourth affirmation: *I am getting better.* Or, *It doesn't have to be scary to heal.*

Here is another example:
Current belief: *I am not forgivable.*
Desired belief: *I am forgivable.*
First affirmation: *It may be possible that I can forgive myself for this.*

Once the first affirmation is accepted and believed, you can take the affirmation one step further.

Second affirmation: *It's possible that I can forgive myself for this.*

Be gentle with yourself. Have compassion even for the process of deciding to have compassion!

Once you have this, move on to the next affirmation.
Third affirmation: *I deserve forgiveness for this.*
Fourth affirmation: *I can forgive myself.* And so on.

These are just examples to help you see the process. Your affirmations will be tailored to what fits for you. Each next affirmation will depend on what is going on for you in the moment. Keep making affirmations that get you gradually closer to the place you would like to be. Take small steps, as small as you need, then bigger when you're ready. There is no finite number of steps that you are going for.

Affirmations are easy. It's so simple to make big, lasting changes to your heart and mind. I'm excited for you to feel the peace and serenity they bring. It's time to let go. You know it is — that's why you're here. Just give yourself a hug for being here. Remember, compassion is the key. You deserve it to be free.

Take action

Ask yourself:

What do I want to move past?

_____

_____

What do I want to let go?

_____

_____

What negative thing do I think about myself?

_____

_____

Preventing the Return of Anxiety

Keep practicing everything in this book. Some people abandon their practices once they feel better. This isn't wise. These practices are important for *maintaining* well-being, too.

I haven't had anxiety in a long, long time, but I still practice the suggestions I share in this book every day. I've gotten used to them and they're second nature by now. I haven't stopped taking care of myself through nourishment, self-compassion, taking a step back, scheduling downtime, getting sleep, meditating, being creative and fostering positive relationships. These all have benefits beyond preventing anxiety.

My practice, my skills, my trust in myself, my understandings about fear and anxiety, and the people I surround myself with are my team to prevent anxiety in the future. This doesn't mean I will never feel fear again. When I'm in danger, it'll be there. I welcome fear's role in keeping me safe and attentive. I'm also grateful of guilt's role in keeping me accountable and committed to being the best person I can be. But I never want to go down the rabbit hole of anxiety or get immobilized by guilt and shame again.

Once my clients have recovered from their anxiety and panic, they always wonder what to do if it comes back. Anxiety has been part of your life for a long time. If you feel a sensation that your amygdala connects with anxious feelings, it will automatically respond. Like with Leslie in Skill #11: Believe You Can — you can change this by immediately talking to yourself in a calming way each time you're triggered by the stimuli. This has to be repeated until the stimulus doesn't affect your brain the same way. Adding action like walking, talking or doing something helps increase the GABA (the hormone that stops the stress hormones) and speeds the healing process.

Another way to hurry the process along is by stimulating yourself on purpose. Because re-training the brain takes repetition, the more often you do it, the faster it goes. Like we did with Jill in Skill #8: Exposure — by watching videos of people throwing up. Doing this gently and taking small steps is best, building up to something harder when you're ready.

When anxiety comes back, it's the meaning you make around those first feelings that's going to affect the intensity of it return-ing. If you feel anxious and you say, "OMG! It's coming back. This is going to be horrible! How am I going to do this? It didn't work. I can't get rid of it!" panic will ensue and spiral out of control.

On the other hand, if you feel anxious and you say, "Okay, I've felt this before. I can handle it. I must have be tired, I'd better get more sleep and take care of myself. This will be gone by tomorrow. Let me distract myself to help it pass faster," you will have a whole different experience.

Review and keep practicing the suggestions in Skill #10: Nourish Yourself. Most important, keep an active lifestyle with exercise and a creative activity as part of your routine.

This book is your touchstone. Your best help for yourself is to pick up *You 1, Anxiety 0* and review. Anxiety repeats itself over and over, so don't get discouraged when you have to repeat the recovery message over and over. You can easily read a section or two related to how you are feeling. Or reread through some of the answers you've made at the end of the sections.

Remember there is no "I" in T-E-A-M. Anxiety wants you isolated, so you do the opposite. If you want a safe community to talk with others like you, join mine online.

jodiaman.com

facebook.com/jodiamanlove

Instagram @jodiamanlove

YouTube Jodi Aman

Twitter @JodiAman

Pinterest JodiAman

Thank you so much for giving your recovery time and attention. You deserve to be happy and free. Go out there and have an adventure.

About the Author

Jodi Aman knows people. She is a practicing psychotherapist who has worked with 35 people a week for 20 years in Rochester, NY. She got her Master's in Science in Social Work from Columbia University in 1996 and has studied and taught Narrative Therapy around the world focusing on trauma and anxiety recovery.

Jodi films and edits her own YouTube channel and has five online courses with a focus on getting rid of anxiety and empowering people to have more joy in their lives. She plays herself in *The Secrets of the Keys* self-help movie.

Jodi knows anxiety. In her youth she was immobilized by her own panic and anxiety, yet she clawed her way back to life, and taught herself to master happiness. In this bestselling book *You 1, Anxiety 0,* she shows readers how to win their life back from fear and panic, helping them find peace in their days.

As an inspirational speaker, she helps audiences make sense of their lives. She shows how to shift thinking, change unwanted situations, and finally stop the out-of-control downward spiral by releasing that internal self-critic.

Do you want to go deeper with Jodi?

Find out how to work with with her at <u>jodiaman.com</u>

Click "Work with me" at the top!

Anxiety-Free Me!

5 week comprehensive online anxiety recovery program!

- Group coaching so it is personalized to YOU.
- Connect with a community that lifts you up and understands.
- Learn what anxiety is and why it is so powerful.
- Get practical tips on how to take it down.
- Change the triggers in your brain.
- Find your life purpose. Find yourself.
- Improve your relationships.
- Live happy and at peace.
- 40+ videos, audios and handouts - for life.

Get it here: jodiaman.com/anxiety-training

Anxiety-Free Kids!

Online anxiety recovery
for parents and kids!

- Immediate access to over 20 videos, audios and fun handouts for you and your child, for life.

- Find out exactly what to do when you can't stand to see your child suffer anymore!

- Kid-friendly videos featuring my baby girl, Miss Lily Aman!

- Hear directly from the horse's mouth as I interview Anxiety herself!

- Access to a private FB group and get support from people who know what you are going through.

- Have fun and feel freedom from anxiety!

Get it here: jodiaman.com/anxiety-training

Driving Anxiety Help

Drive relaxed and in control!

- Feel in control when you drive.
- Drive your family to places where you'd get to spend quality time and create memories.
- Don't miss another party - no matter which part of town it's in!
- Go to that concert or convention with your friends.
- Get to work without the stress.
- Six downloadable mp3s to listen to while you are driving.
- Build a sturdy self-confidence.

Get it here: jodiaman.com/anxiety-training

Flying Free From Fear

Get rid of flying anxiety with this meditation series.

- Three mp3s to prepare you for your flight.
- Eight more to use while you are flying.
- Start your recovery as soon as you book your trip.
- Feel in control before you fly.
- Put your family first and your fear last.
- Don't miss or avoid another adventure.
- Have more fun in your life.
- See those ancient ruins!
- Fly to whatever you want.

Get it here: jodiaman.com/anxiety-training